IMMERSION

THE DIO TRILOGY - BOOK 2

Jared Dodd

The DIO Trilogy Book Series:

Discipleship
Immersion
Obedience

Immersion - The DIO Trilogy Book 2

Copyright © 2013

Jared Dodd

Scripture quotations are from The Holy Bible, English Standard Version, copyright ©2001 by Crossway Bibles, a publishing ministry of Good News Publishers. Used by permission. All rights reserved.

All rights reserved. No part of this document may be reproduced, stored in a retrieval system, or transmitted in any form or by any means; electronic, mechanical, photocopy, recording, or otherwise; without the permission of the author.

First Edition - Printed in the U.S.A.

Special Thanks to:

Pastor, and friend, Luke Dye and the saints at White Stone Community Church- Together we unraveled the mysteries of discipleship. God be praised.

My wife, Amy- for all the time you put into formatting this volume. Thank you.

Amy Kayser and Jimmy Dodd- who edited this book. Thank you.

My God and King- There is not one good thing in my life that I can take credit for. Everything I have and do and am is completely because of You.

Thank You.

Table of Contents

How to Use This book 1
Chapter 1- Baptism 3
Chapter 2- Abba 15
Chapter 3- Provider 31
Chapter 4- Protector 43
Chapter 5- Creator 55
Chapter 6- Brother 67
Chapter 7- Savior 77
Chapter 8- King 89
Chapter 9- Judge 101
Chapter 10- The Head Of The Body 111
Chapter 11- The Holy Spirit 125

HOW TO USE THIS BOOK

This manuscript is Book Two in The DIO Trilogy. It yields the best results when done in a small group of believers that is led by a teacher who has experienced much of the immersion process described in this book. Your level of success will not only depend on your comprehension of the things mentioned, but even more so the practice of them.

The Purpose of The DIO Trilogy is to assist the church in fulfilling the Great Commission by first living the Great Commission. The second mandate of the Great Commission is to be baptized. The aim of this book is to explore what baptism is and how to experience it.

There are various disciplines offered within this volume which can be found at the end of each chapter. A journal will be necessary to rightly engage in these disciplines. They are as follows:

- Main Points
- Questions to consider
- The Discipline of Study
- The Discipline of Memorization
- The Discipline of Meditation
- The Discipline of Prayer
- Breath Prayers

I would highly encourage all who undertake this study to give themselves fully, not only to the writings, but also to the disciplines.

All questions and comments are gladly welcomed at jared@thedioproject.org. Blessings upon you, your families, and all of God's Church.

THE GREAT COMMISSION

"Then Jesus came to them and said, "All authority in heaven and on earth has been given to me. Therefore go and make <u>disciples</u> of all nations, <u>baptizing</u> them in the name of the Father and of the Son and of the Holy Spirit, and teaching them to <u>obey</u> everything I have commanded you. And surely I am with you always, to the very end of the age."

Matthew 28:18-20

CHAPTER 1

BAPTISM

> ""I do not ask for these only, but also for those who will believe in me through their word, that they may all be one, just as you, Father, are in me, and I in you, that they also may be in us, so that the world may believe that you have sent me."
>
> -- John 17:20-21

It's only moments before Jesus' betrayal. He knows that all His friends, whom He was feasting with earlier that evening, will soon abandon Him. He is tired and weak, and the overwhelming sorrow in His heart is causing Him to sweat drops of blood. Even raising His face to the heavens is difficult. He knows that His torture is nigh. And yet, somehow, He is able to see through the oncoming torment and intercede for mankind. And what was His prayer? *That they also may be in us…*

It should greatly comfort you to think that two thousand years ago, on the night of His betrayal, Jesus was praying for you. He prayed that you would not merely know about Him, but moreover, that you would be in Him. God wants such an intimate union with His followers that He invites us to dwell within His person.

> "Go and make followers of all peoples, immersing them in the Father and the Son and the Holy Spirit..."
>
> Matthew 28:19 (paraphrase)

God wants us to be immersed in Him. But we don't begin with immersion. Immersion is not step one, rather it is step two. Trying to immerse someone into God without them first being a disciple is impossible. Discipleship comes first; baptism second. Only the apprentice of Christ is ready and able to be immersed into God.

RETHINKING BAPTISM

Everyone has heard the word **baptism**, and therefore has an idea, or doctrine, associated with it. For some it is a symbol of turning over a new leaf. For others, it is a necessary step in becoming a member of a certain church or religion. Theologians debate over whether people should be sprinkled or dunked when baptized. Others see baptism as something only for adults while others insist that infants can and should be baptized. These are questions that should be answered. Yet even when answered correctly, it is still very possible to misunderstand the kind of baptism which Jesus originally intended.

We need to rethink baptism. For my own journey, this meant forgetting virtually everything I thought I knew about baptism and beginning afresh with the scriptures and Holy Spirit alone as my guide. One of the best prayers I ever prayed was, *God, erase everything I think I know.* This might be a necessary step in your own spiritual pilgrimage.

The word *baptism* comes from the Greek word *baptizo*. This word literally means *to immerse*. In Jesus' day it was a word used in many different contexts, one of which was the dying of cloth. The dyer would take the white cloth and baptize, or immerse it, in the colored dye. The cloth would then take on all of the properties of the dye. We see in this context that to baptize the cloth meant not only to immerse it, but also included the idea of it being permeated by the dye. The cloth ended up looking just like the dye. I believe that this is God's will for us: **He wants us to be put into Him so that we can be like Him**. Paul speaks of this immersion in his letter to the Christians at Rome:

> "Do you not know that all of us who have been baptized into Christ Jesus were baptized into his death? We were buried therefore with him by baptism into death, in order that, just as Christ was raised from the dead by the glory of the Father, we too might walk in newness of life. For if we have been united with him in a death like his, we shall certainly be united with him in a resurrection like his."
>
> Romans 6:3-5

The word *baptize* here often brings about confusion when we think it's strictly speaking of water baptism. Paul is not speaking here of water baptism alone, but is instead stating that at the beginning of our salvation we were put, or immersed, into Christ. We were also therefore immersed in His death, burial, and resurrection. It is like he says in verse six: **we have been <u>united</u> with him**. This unity, this oneness, comes from us being immersed in the person of God. It may be helpful to reread the verses above, inserting the word *immersed* in the place of *baptized*.

We must understand though, that even though we are immersed in Christ through faith in Him, water baptism is still something that we are commanded to do. It is a symbol of our unity with Christ that comes through faith. We are identified with His death, burial, and resurrection. God wants all people to acknowledge this and submit to His commandment to become disciples, and then be baptized. It is important to remember that there is an order to this. Baptism is for disciples. If you were baptized as an infant, or anytime in your life before you were a disciple, and are now wondering if as a disciple you should baptized, my advice to you would be to follow the commands of Christ. Be a disciple who is then baptized.

The point that I want to make is that baptism goes well beyond water. John the Baptist understood this principle. (From his name alone, it seems that he understood a lot about baptism). Consider the passage below:

> "John answered them all, saying, "I baptize you with water, but he who is mightier than I is coming, the strap of whose sandals I am not worthy to untie. He will baptize you with the Holy Spirit and with fire. His winnowing fork is in his hand, to clear his threshing floor and to gather the wheat into his barn, but the chaff he will burn with unquenchable fire."
>
> *Luke 3:16,17*

John explains to us that there are many different things to be immersed in. He immersed people in water. Jesus came, however, not to immerse people in water, but rather in either His Spirit or the fires of hell. These are the only two options for humans today. (Many people fail to see this because they think that all baptisms must be good). According to John, we can either be baptized in God or we can be baptized in the Lake of Fire. God's will is that we would become disciples, thereby immersing ourselves in Him.

The focus of this book is to understand that baptism does not end with being dunked into water. Water baptism is important and good, but it is only the beginning of our baptism, not the end. Most of the church today, with their best intentions of course, views the Great Commission as a very quick and easy checklist. ***Get someone to believe that Jesus died, check. Dunk them in the water, check. Wow! That only took five minutes!*** We must rightly see instead that the Great Commission is a process that carries on throughout our lifetime. The starting lines are faith and water baptism, and they are wonderful. But what has happened today is that most of us have viewed the starting line as the finish line and have therefore set the church into a perpetual cycle of spiritual infancy.

Jesus' instruction given to His first band of followers was to make disciples and then immerse them in the Father and the Son and the Holy Spirit. God is inviting us to practically step into the reality of His love, light, and Spirit. Peter rightly understood that this idea of being baptized was not second to the gospel, but was rather an instrumental part of Jesus' Good News.

> "His divine power has granted to us all things that pertain to life and godliness, through the knowledge of him who called us to his own glory and excellence, by which he has granted to us his precious and very great promises, so that through them you may become partakers of the divine nature, having escaped from the corruption that is in the world because of sinful desire."
>
> 2 Peter 1:3-4

Peter explained that we have been given ***everything we need for life and godliness***. This is a message that desperately needs to be preached today. Too many Christians think that they are without proper provisions for holiness, and are therefore set up for failure in regards to the Christian life. We are indeed able, according to the verse above, to *escape the corruption in the world*. This is the Good News of Jesus Christ! We don't have to wait until death to reign with God. We can have victory today. We have been given everything we need to escape the darkness of Satan's kingdom. And yet, according to verse four, how do we escape the corruption of this world? We escape corruption by *participating in the divine nature*. Peter rightly understood that the only opportunity given to us to experience freedom from sin is God Himself. What does it mean to be immersed in God? It means to participate in His divine nature. *It means to walk in light of the fact of who God is.* Notice also that this provision of freedom comes through our knowledge of God. This is not mere head knowledge of God, but rather an interactive relationship, much like that between two spouses. When I married my wife I did not walk away from the altar that day thinking that I had completed my quest of marriage. I rather understood that the adventure had just begun. When we choose to cross the line into discipleship with Christ we have only begun the journey; we have made our first step upon the narrow path, and now the invitation that our Heavenly Spouse gives us is to immerse ourselves in Him. He is in essence saying to us, *Now you are finally able to experience Me and know Me and be active with Me. Come! Dive in! You will never reach the bottom of my being. There will always be more of me to find! And the more of Me you find, the better your experience in My Kingdom will be!*

This is the journey that Jesus commands us to take: that all disciples be immersed into the name, or reality, of God. Something we must understand is the amazing power of the names *Father, Son, and Holy Spirit*. God could have said that we are to dive into the God of love, power, grace, etc. But, instead of His characteristics, He gives us the greatest revelation of His name: He is Father. He is Son. He is Holy Spirit. Within these names are an endless array of blessing and transformation for the disciple who chooses to obediently and lovingly and humbly immerse himself within them. This is the purpose of this second book. We are going to immerse ourselves into God. We will only scratch the surface, but in the end we will be equipped and hopefully inspired to venture on.

THE CHALLENGE

All of us are immersed in something. In order for us to dive into God we must first remove ourselves from whatever else we have been immersed in. These might be very obvious things such as addictions (both physical and mental). For most people however, worldly immersion doesn't seem dangerous or distracting. Things such as entertainment, careers, food, and hobbies are some of the things that, even though they aren't bad in and of themselves, have become our god. The challenge given here is to pull out of these activities to create room for God to be your focus. Unplug your television for a few days, or even weeks. Refrain from any late night snacks that are so easy to run to when we feel bored or worn down. Say no to anything sports-related for a season. What you'll find is that an incredible chasm will be opened within you, and you will be much more receptive to experience God. You may come back to some of these activities in the future. Some of them however, will be rendered as unworthy of your time. You can only occupy yourself with so much. I would encourage you to only choose those things worthy of a disciple.

The practical instruction for how we actually do this immersion into God is quite simple, especially when we consider how we immerse ourselves in this world. If someone wants to be immersed in this world they will follow a simple plan. They will choose to be educated in the principles of this world, such as greed and lust. They will then meditate on these things, continually deepening their faith in believing that the best thing they can do is chase after wealth and pleasure. This conviction will result in frequent pursuit and practice. They will participate with the world in this agenda, continually allowing their experience to validate and strengthen their deep-rooted philosophy of worldliness. All of us, to some degree, have done this in our own life. We simply need to apply the same principles and logic to the Kingdom of God. We must first learn the realities of who God is. We must meditate on them, believe in them, and choose to participate in who He is. And as we immerse ourselves more in Him, we will naturally be taken more and more out of the vanity of this world and put into the experience of God and His Kingdom. You have a God who is very near to you. He is able to do more than you can imagine. He made you and loves you more than anything else. He is continually giving you good things, moment by moment, as you live your life. He is offering you shelter from the storms of this world by drawing you away from sin so you can obey His word. And all the while He is bidding you to come and share in His very being. He wants you to know Him as one knows a bride or a groom. This is His will for you. A certain poet recently wrote, *Take me into the Beautiful.* That is what we are going to do. We begin with the Father.

END NOTES:

Main Points:

- Baptize = immerse.
- To immerse ourselves into God means to live life in light of the fact of who God is.
- Everyone is immersed in something.
- Baptism into God is a life-long process.

Questions to Consider:

- How has this chapter challenged or changed some of your ideas concerning baptism?
- When you take an honest look at your life, in what ways do you see more of an immersion in the world? How do you see more of an immersion in the Kingdom of God?

The Discipline of Study:

Read John 17:20-26. This is a prayer that Jesus prayed on the night before His crucifixion and He prayed it for you! Record any observations/questions as you answer the questions below:

- According to Jesus' prayer, what will be some of the results of us being immersed in Him?
- According to Jesus' words, why is the church so divided today?
- According to Jesus's words, why does He make His Father known?

The Discipline of Meditation:

Meditate on 2 Peter 1:3-4. Read through it slowly, and try to let the words soak into your heart. Say to yourself repeatedly, *In Him, I have everything I need.* Thank God for the amazing reality that He has given you everything you need for godly living. Meditate on the phrase *you may participate in the divine nature.* Say this over and over and allow God to inspire you that this is an amazing opportunity that has been given to you.

The Discipline of Memorization:

John 17:23-24

> "I in them and you in me. May they be brought to complete unity to let the world know that you sent me and have loved them even as you have loved me.
>
> "Father, I want those you have given me to be with me where I am, and to see my glory, the glory you have given me because you loved me before the creation of the world."

The Discipline of Prayer:

Holy Father, I thank you that you have invited me to submerge myself into your Being. I pray that I would dive into You, and in doing so, experience the life for which You created me. Help me to pull myself out of the darkness of this world that I might enter into you. Don't allow me to miss out on this opportunity. Thank you that You are Father, and Son, and Holy Spirit. Amen.

CHAPTER 2

ABBA

> *"For you did not receive a spirit that makes you a slave again to fear, but you received the Spirit of sonship. And by him we cry, "Abba, Father."*
>
> --Romans 8:15

There are no orphans in the Kingdom of God. Every person in His Kingdom, everyone who belongs to Him, is a son. This is because of the requirement for citizenship in the Kingdom. Every kingdom has its requirements for citizenship, and in God's Kingdom, every citizen must be a son. Jesus spoke of this with Nicodemus when He said, "No one can see the Kingdom of God unless He is born again." Just as God breathed life into Adam, so must God breathe spiritual life into those who will inherit His dominion.

In the beginning, Adam was God's son (Luke 3:38). He spoke with His Father, learned from His Father, and took part in His Father's work. When Adam sinned, mankind lost their sonship and became orphans in this world, or worse yet, sons of the evil one. It has, therefore, always been God's objective to bring people back into the father-son relationship for which they were created.

In Book One of this series, we discussed how important it is for us to fulfill our God-given mandate to rule. What we must now realize is that the context within which we rule is that of sons of God. We were never intended to rule with God as orphans or slaves or peasants. We rule as sons of the Most High.

> "So you are no longer a slave, but a son; and since you are a son, God has made you also an heir."
>
> Galatians 4:7

This is what separates God's Kingdom from every other nation or kingdom on this earth. In God's Kingdom, all citizens are heirs. They are all princes of the King. If you are a citizen of God's Kingdom, then you are a son and therefore carry with you the authority of your Father King. This is without a doubt the greatest and most important aspect of our relationship with God. He is Father, we are sons. This is the context in which we walk with God. Without this understanding we will live as orphans and will therefore not be able to appropriate our full rights as sons.

As a son of God you have all of His Kingdom available to you. You have been '*blessed with all spiritual blessings in Christ*' (Ephesians 1:3). All of His love, power, wisdom, and blessing are at your fingertips. All that lacks is the next step of maturity. As you grow in Him as His son, He will entrust you with more of His Kingdom. This is the process of growing as a son of God, and is very much like the instructing, entrusting, and molding of your own children. Let this truth encourage you greatly. God sees you as His child. He wants you to see Him as your Father.

Imagine if your earthly father was King of this world. What would you lack? What would you worry about? What would you fear? Nothing! This is the reality of our citizenship in the Kingdom of God. Our Heavenly Father is

King and He wants us to never stop growing in our understanding as we experience this all-encompassing relationship.

It is very common tradition in the church today to call God our Father. Every time we begin what is commonly referred to as 'The Lord's Prayer', we begin with these words: *Our Father*. This is good, for it is what Jesus taught us to say. In our modern culture, however, we don't often use the word 'father' in reference to our paternal parent. My children don't call me father, but instead they call me daddy. This is what God wants for us. He wants to be our daddy. He wants an intimacy and a relationship much like my relationship with my children. He wants us to pray: *Our Daddy, who is in heaven...* (I'm not saying it's wrong to call Him *Father*, but am rather addressing the attitude of our heart. We need to look to God as a child looks to their dad.)

This is the kind of relationship Jesus had with His Heavenly Father. It's interesting to note that when Jesus' need for God was most dire, He cried out to His Father with the Aramaic term **Abba**. Abba would best be translated today as **Papa** or **Daddy**. This is why God put within us who believe the Spirit of sonship (Romans 8:15). It is what makes us able to call God our Abba. It is what gives us the right to raise our hands up to our Heavenly Daddy much like our little children will raise their hands to us when they want us to pick them up and hold them close.

Jesus demonstrated for us this kind of relationship when He walked this earth. He came to show us the Father and to show us what it looked like for a son to follow His Abba.

"Righteous Father, though the world does not know you, I know you, and they know that you have sent me.

> <u>I have made you known to them, and will continue to make you known</u> in order that the love you have for me may be in them and that I myself may be in them."
>
> *John 17:25-26*

God wanted mankind to know Him as Father. This was part of Jesus' mission. And as we learned in Book One, Jesus is not finished carrying out that mission. He is still making His Father known today. You might say, "Well, I know God my Father, so Jesus is finished making His Father known to me." But we must remember what Jesus meant when He used the word *'know'*. He didn't mean to simply know about the Father, but rather to know Him intimately, or to have an interactive relationship with Him. He wanted you to have a father/son relationship with your God that is stronger than anything you've ever experienced. This is not a onetime thing, but rather a process that I believe will continue for all eternity. Consider your own family. Most parents desire to have a relationship with their child that is real and intimate. We are not content with our children simply knowing us as someone who lives in the same vicinity and puts food on the table and sometimes says, 'Have a nice day.' We want our kids to know us very well, and to know our immense love for them. We want to spend time with them as they love us and obey us. We want to teach them things and open their eyes to wonderful aspects of God and life. This is what God wants. He wants to be more to us than just that great guy in the sky who gives us cool stuff and takes us to heaven. One thing I can promise you is that however much you know God, and however much you have a real intimate relationship with Him, He has more of Himself to show you. You and I will never be at a spot where there is no more of God to learn and experience as Father. He wants us to look to Him as a young child looks to their daddy. He wants us to live life with Him as a little child would.

Jesus spoke of this often. One of the most insightful teachings of Jesus on this subject, which is often overlooked, is found in the account of Matthew.

> "And he said: "I tell you the truth, unless you change and become like little children, you will never enter the kingdom of heaven."
>
> *Matthew 18:3*

The two words that should initially catch our attention are unless and never. Jesus is saying here that unless we change and become like little children, that we will never enter His Kingdom. Do you want to enter the kingdom of heaven? If so, this verse should be of top priority to both understand and apply. Jesus says that we must change. You and I cannot stay the same. Do you think that there is a need for change in your life? I know there certainly is in mine. We need to change. We need to stop thinking the way this world has trained us to think. Jesus explains this change in the second half of this verse.

Not only does Jesus say we must change but we must also ***become***. We must ***become like little children***. This is how we escape the thinking of this world; we become like little children. (Doesn't sound much like the great strategies of the church today, does it?) Notice that Jesus says that we must become like *little* children. These are children who are still at the age where they, like Jesus, refer to their Father as *daddy*. This is one of the initial ways that we immerse ourselves in God the Father. We see Him as our Daddy, and therefore interact with Him as such. We live each day in light of the fact that our Dad is King of the universe.

How do our little children immerse themselves in the activity of their earthly fathers? How do they take full advantage of the relationship? The answer is simple. ***They believe everything their dad says.*** As of today, I have five children. They still see me as daddy and ***believe everything I tell them***, therefore experiencing the immense blessings of such a relationship. If I tell them that there is a large man dressed in red who lives at the North Pole, who is able to visit everyone in one night, guess what? They believe me without any doubt. (I don't tell my children this, but it is a powerful example.) I have told my children that I will always feed them and care for them and they believe me without any doubt. Their faith does not require proof or understanding of any kind; all they need is the word of their daddy. This is likewise what we are to do with our Heavenly Father. Without this immersion, we will not experience His Kingdom, for it is a Kingdom that is built upon faith in the invisible.

Being like little children, therefore, is to **believe everything my Abba says _He did_**. Our Heavenly Father says that He created the universe in six days. As His children, we don't need any explanation or evidence (even though the evidence is vast). All we need is the word of our Heavenly Daddy. You see, this is to live completely contrary to the thinking of this world. Most of us are immersed in this world. We act like it acts. We believe what it says. We live like it lives. We require proof for everything, continually walking according to the principles of humanism and realism. And yet, we don't have to live this way. We can live as little children of God who walk completely contrary to the thinking of this world. The choice is ours. We can either be baptized in the thinking of this world, and therefore look like the world, or we can be baptized in our God and therefore look like Him. It's up to us, and the consequences on both sides are eternal.

Little children also believe **everything daddy says _about himself_**. Our Father says that He is able to do anything. What would our lives look like if we really believed this with all our heart, as a little child would? We would stand firm, even if our circumstances seemed to contradict God's word. It wouldn't matter because we would believe what our Daddy told us. We would believe that He can do anything. God also tells us that He knows all things; He is the smartest person in the world. He holds all the answers. He is also the epitome of love and truth and holiness. That is who your Abba is, and He desires for you to immerse yourself in this reality so that you might believe it and participate in it with every fiber of your being. As we've mentioned before: in order to follow God correctly, you must know Him correctly.

Children also believe *what dad says about who they are*. Do you believe your Father's words concerning who you are? He says that you are wonderfully made. He says that He has plans for you that are greater than you could ever imagine. I tell my daughter that she is beautiful and she believes me. Why? Because she is a little child who trusts her father. If we don't believe what our Father says about us then we haven't become like little children. This is a huge area of warfare today. This world bombards us with an identity that is completely opposed to the Bible and God's words to us. Unfortunately, despite our best efforts and study, we still buy into the lie of the enemy. We continue to make our greatest priority our physical appearance or our amount of knowledge instead of listening to our Father's words. We still look to the words of others for validation instead of the words of our Dad. The pain and captivity due to this is staggering. What is the cure? According to Jesus, it is to change and become like little children.

Lastly, our Father tells *us the best way to live life*. He says that we are to aim for pleasing Him, and that it is better to store our treasures in heaven than on earth. He says to love our enemies and give to those who are in need. As little children we are able to believe this without any further proof or explanation. We are not looking for the world to agree with us. We are able to walk within this world confident of the realities of God's Kingdom. Who do you look to as your authority on how to live life? Abba doesn't just know what is best for the afterlife, but also for life today.

This is what it means to immerse ourselves in our Abba. It is to live with a certain attitude. *It is to walk in light of the fact that our Dad is King of the universe*. What would your mind-set be if your biological dad was in charge of planet Earth and owned an endless amount of possessions? When you would walk into a building, or when you would get up to speak, you would do it with an attitude that understood who you are. Likewise, we are to live life from an understanding and attitude of someone whose daddy is God. This is not just a mental understanding, but something that transforms our very soul. This is what

Peter was speaking of when he said that we are able to ***participate in the divine nature***. Your Daddy in heaven is loving you, providing for you, giving you truth and identity, as well as revealing Himself to you. It is up to you to immerse yourself in Him. If you do, you will experience something greater than anything this world has to offer.

> "Do not be afraid, little flock, for your Father has been pleased to give you the kingdom."
>
> Luke 12:32

THE EXAMPLE OF JESUS

> "But a time is coming, and has come, when you will be scattered, each to his own home. You will leave me all alone. Yet I am not alone, for my Father is with me."
>
> John 16:32

> …but the world must learn that I love the Father and that I do exactly what my Father has commanded me."
>
> John 14:31

Just as a young child will imitate his father, Jesus imitated His Father perfectly. He believed all that His Father said, and the result was the most amazing life ever exemplified to mankind. Jesus' mind was continually focused on the person of His Father. He lived life continually practicing the presence of His Father. He trusted His Father, and because He trusted Him, He loved Him. Jesus knew that His Father was ever with Him. He was never alone. The reason that Jesus' life is so amazing is because He immersed Himself in His Abba. If we want His results, we must do what He did.

THE CHALLENGE

For many people in this world, the idea of "father" brings many negative connotations to both mind and spirit. This is due to the fact that many people have been abused, neglected, criticized, and abandoned by the people they called *daddy*. If this is you, I want to begin by saying how sorry I am for your pain. I also want to assure you that this was never God's intention. God did not choose for your dad to be the way he was, or still is today. That was your dad's choice, and I pity him for his actions. God wants to show you what a daddy is supposed to look like in the person of Himself. This invitation will likely be very scary for you. It's okay, God knows this. He is a patient and gentle Father. And He loves you more than anything else in this world.

The first step to experiencing God as your Father is to come to the point where you are able to forgive your earthly father. This doesn't mean that you have to forget what happened. It doesn't mean that you have to like what happened. It simply means that you are willing to say in your heart, ***I forgive you for the wrong you did to me***. This can often be a very difficult and challenging thing to do, but I want to assure you that you will be glad that you did it. Forgiveness is powerful. After you forgive your earthly father you will be ready to embrace your Heavenly Father. Here is a prayer that you may want to pray:

> Dear Heavenly Father. I pray that you would help me forgive my earthly father with all of my heart. I choose now to forgive him, just as you also have forgiven him. And I pray now that I could learn anew, from You, what it means to be your son/daughter and for you to be my

Daddy. I pray that You would help me to trust in You and to run to You and to hide myself in You. Thank you so much for making me your child. Thank you so so so much for making me your son/daughter. Amen.

END NOTES:

Main Points:

- To immerse myself in my Abba I must change and become like a little child.
- To immerse myself in my Abba I must believe all that He says is true about Himself, me, and life.

Questions to Consider:

- Are there things your Abba says about Himself that you don't believe?
- Are there things your Abba says about you that you don't believe?
- Are there things that your Abba says about how to live life that you don't believe?

The Discipline of Study:

Look up the following passages and read them as a child would. Answer the corresponding questions:

Psalm 139:1-16

- According to this passage, what is true about you?
- Is there any place that you can go where your Father won't follow?
- How does this passage encourage you? What truths about you and God stand out the most?

Luke 12:22-34

- Why do you never need to worry?

- What should your focus be?
- Meditate on verse 32. How does this verse challenge your thinking?

The Discipline of Meditation:

Imagine being a child again, except this time you live in God's house and God is your Father. Picture sitting at the kitchen table as He makes you breakfast and speaks with you about His love for you and how wonderful you are. Imagine Him taking you where you need to go and making sure that you have everything you need. Imagine Him tucking you in bed at night and telling you stories and praying over you and kissing you good night. (Take your time with this one.)

Now meditate on the fact that this is God's heart for you. It is also a perfect picture of what you can experience in the spiritual realm on a daily basis with God. Thank Him that He loves you as His son.

The Discipline of Memorization:

Matthew 18:3

> "And he said: "I tell you the truth, unless you change and become like little children, you will never enter the kingdom of heaven."

Luke 12:32

> "Do not be afraid, little flock, for your Father has been pleased to give you the kingdom."

The Discipline of Prayer:

Dear Daddy, thank you for being my Dad and loving me with all of your heart. Help me change and become like a little child. Help me to trust in you and believe your precious promises. From morning until night, may I daily run to you as my Dad. When You speak, help me to believe without any doubt and with zero hesitation. When You tell me who I am, may I listen to You instead of the world. May I continually remain cradled upon your lap, safe within Your arms. Amen.

CHAPTER 3

PROVIDER

"His divine power has given us everything we need for life and godliness..."

--2 Peter 1:3

"Give us today our daily bread."

--Matthew 6:11

We are, by nature, needy people. We need physical sustenance, emotional stability, and spiritual life. Something we must understand at the onset is that having these needs is a good thing, for it is the way God made us. He made us to need food and drink, clothing and shelter, community and love. The reality of our need is not a weakness, but rather an amazing opportunity to find our provision in God alone. God, your Heavenly Father, desires to provide for your needs in abundance. He desires for you to look to Him from when you awaken each morning to when you fall asleep in the evening. This is the amazing opportunity you have to immerse ourselves in **God your Provider**.

The world, by way of contrast, is in constant pursuit of meeting their needs outside the person of Jesus Christ. Instead of running to Christ, the world pursues things such as hobbies, work, sinful activity, and relationships in attempt to satisfy their God-given necessities. All of us have experienced this, and have hopefully concluded that the attempts of this world to meet these needs are far from sufficient. They may meet them to a degree, but they will never fulfill our needs in the way that only God and His Kingdom can. Let me say it again loud and clear: **This world, in and of itself, cannot truly meet our spiritual, emotional, and physical needs**. The love of this world is not real love. The peace of this world is not true peace. They are imitations, bearing some resemblance to God's provision, but falling very short from loving as God loves and providing the peace that surpasses all understanding. Regarding our physical needs, this world can meet them to an extent, but not the way originally intended, for God's plan was that we would receive our sustenance with a heart of thankfulness to our Heavenly Provider.

God is your Provider. Every day He offers to you everything you need physically, emotionally, and spiritually. And He is also inviting you to participate with Him in His provision. How do we immerse ourselves in God as our Provider? We immerse ourselves in Him by **being thankful**. As He provides for you moment by moment you are able to respond with thanksgiving. This may sound too simple, but don't be deceived; it is extremely powerful and life changing. This is why the Scripture says that we are to be thankful always. Have you ever considered the power of thankfulness? If ever you find yourself to be discontent, nine times out of ten it can be traced back to a lack of thankfulness. To be thankful is to acknowledge God by focusing on the good He has given us instead of focusing on what we consider to be the negative aspects of our circumstance.

> "Don't be deceived, my dear brothers. Every good and perfect gift is from above, coming down from the

Father of the heavenly lights, who does not change like shifting shadows."

James 1:16-17

According to this passage ***every*** good thing we receive in this life comes to us from our Father, even if we don't recognize it as such. The goal of this chapter is that we would recognize our Father's gifts and respond with thanksgiving. Note also that these gifts are not only good, some of them are perfect. God's perfect gifts of salvation and His Word are just a few of these presents. The greatest gift of course being His Holy Spirit that He gives to those who believe in Him.

SEEING THE SIMPLE THINGS

Have you ever considered all the gifts that God gives us? We are quick to list wonderful things such as salvation, love, forgiveness and the like. These are wonderful gifts of God that we take for granted daily. Yet in addition to these, we must also remember to focus upon the simple things. Who gives you the sunshine, or the rain? Who gives you food, fresh air, friendship, and all of your numerous possessions? Try to imagine life without the song of birds, or the sound of the ocean, or laughter, or fresh fruit, or any of things that your five senses enjoy. Think about the hugs and kisses, the running of fingers through a child's hair, chocolate, or going fishing in a quiet place. Every second of every day God allows your hearts to beat. Every breath is a gift from Him. And as He lavishes down His good and perfect gifts you are able to receive them with thankfulness. This simple act will revolutionize your life. You will walk throughout your day in joyful recognition of your Daddy who continually loves you as your Provider. Too often we are the spoiled child that is complaining about the gift not being the right color as we eat our chocolate and sit upon our comfy chair. This, therefore, is one of the differences between the person who is immersed in the world and the person who is immersed in their Father. The disciple of Christ, who is immersed in His Provider, will continually sense the presence of their Supplier. They will continually be filled with a joy that this world can't comprehend. They will see the hand of their God from the moment they open their eyes in the morning until their last thought before they doze off to sleep in the evening. They will continually be overflowing with thankfulness. This should be our goal.

WHAT ABOUT HARD TIMES?

There will certainly be times in our lives when it seems like there is nothing to be thankful for. A very real example of this is the death of a loved one. How can I be thankful when a loved one, especially someone who died very young, is taken from us without any explanation? This is very difficult, and it should be mentioned here that mourning and sadness is not opposed to thanksgiving. It is not a sin to be sad or mournful. Jesus experienced both of these emotions. And it's His desire that we would, like Him, be thankful in all things, even the loss of a loved one. I have never lost a child, so I cannot rightly understand what that would feel like. But I do know that God lost His firstborn Son, and not only that, but He lost His Son by the hands of those He died for. He is able to relate with us in our suffering. This is important to remember.

How do we give thanks in the midst of such circumstances? We can begin by being thankful for the person and the wonderful memories we had together. We can also give thanks for how God used our loved one to open our eyes up to Him, which can continue to happen even after they are gone. Most importantly, we can give thanks for the hope we have in Jesus; the hope that is stronger than the grave.

> "Where, O death, is your victory? Where, O death, is your sting?"
>
> 1 Corinthians 15:55

Death should bring a legitimate grief because of the separation from our loved one. But for those who belong to Christ, this separation is brief. One hundred years from now we will be together, and will remain together in Christ for all of eternity. What an amazing reality to be thankful for!

What about our loved ones who have died and were clearly not children of God? This is a sobering topic. Having conducted funerals within which this was a reality, I have experienced firsthand this predicament. In such circumstances, we can give thanks that Jesus is Lord. He is still good, holy, just, and loving. Even in such a tragedy as the one we are now addressing, in light of the fact that Jesus is Lord, we can still have a thankful heart. As we practice this, God will give us a peace that transcends all understanding.

The ultimate result of thankfulness will be adoration for God. As we give thanks in all things, our heart will overflow with worship for our Abba. How can we adore our Heavenly Father when we are continually criticizing all of His gifts? How can we adore our Heavenly Father when we think like the world does and fail to see His goodness? If we are going to be people of worship, then we must become thankful people.

THE EXAMPLE OF JESUS

Did Jesus ever worry about His needs being met? Likewise, did He ever complain about His circumstances? Jesus lived His life immersed in His Provider, and was therefore completely content and thankful in all things.

> "After taking the cup, he gave thanks and said, "Take this and divide it among you.""
>
> John 22:17

Many read quickly through the account above without realizing the amazing perspective of Christ. There are three words that should completely astonish us, **He gave thanks**. Remember, this meal was only hours before His betrayal, and less than a day before His crucifixion, both of which Jesus knew were coming. And yet, despite the coming pain and abandonment, Jesus is both able and willing to give thanks for a simple sip of wine. He was able to do this because He rightly understood that this small refreshment was given to Him by His Father in Heaven.

THE CHALLENGE

> "Do everything without complaining or arguing…"
>
> Philippians 2:14

If you want to be like Jesus, then you must do what He did. Jesus lived His life constantly immersed in His Provider, and was therefore continually thankful. When you and I choose to complain about our circumstances we are criticizing our Father's provision. We are being spoiled children who need to therefore be chastised by our Father. God's Kingdom does not need more spoiled brats whining the way that the world does. The challenge set before us is to **open our eyes**! How would it affect your life if you were thankful in all things? How would it affect those around you? How would it affect your family? How would it benefit God's Kingdom?

> "...give thanks in all circumstances, for this is God's will for you in Christ Jesus."
>
> *1 Thessalonians 5:18*

Something we need to understand is that circumstances will never change our level of thankfulness. What I mean is, someone might think, 'If only my circumstances would change, then I'd be thankful.' This thinking is very common and it is also very wrong. Circumstances don't make people thankful. True thankfulness, the thankfulness of God's Kingdom, is outside of circumstance. Thankful people are simply thankful in all things, regardless of the situation. If you are waiting for things to change so you can finally be thankful then you need to understand that you will never be thankful. There is always something to complain about, and you will find it. Even if you get that raise you want at work, or even if you get that house you want, your attitude will not change. You will complain about the carpet in your new house and you will whine about not getting the vacation time you wanted.

What we are speaking of in this section is not a suggestion, but rather a command. Giving thanks in **all** circumstances is **God's will for you**! This command is not for God's benefit but for yours. Do you ever wonder what is missing in your life? What if it is something as simple as giving thanks in every circumstance? I love it when my children respond to my provision with thanksgiving, not because it makes me feel good about me, but rather because it gives my children a perspective that sets them up for success in this life. Without a thankful heart, without immersing yourself in your Provider, true life in God's Kingdom will be impossible.

END NOTES:

Main Points:

- God blesses us every day physically, emotionally, and spiritually.
- God commands us to be thankful in all circumstances.
- A thankful heart is a happy heart.
- A thankful heart is a heart ready to be used by God.
- We immerse ourselves in our Abba by being thankful.

Questions to Consider:

- When do you tend to complain?
- Think of a specific example of not being thankful. Looking back, what can you give thanks for?
- How does not being thankful affect your personal kingdom?

The Discipline of Study:

Begin by listing out ten examples in the Bible of God providing for people (there are many more then 10, but try to write down the ones that stand out to you personally). How do these examples of God's provision encourage you?

The Discipline of Meditation:

1. Begin by being still for a few minutes. Focus on the Father's presence with you.

2. Now meditate on the verse in James 1:16-17:

   > "Don't be deceived, my dear brothers. Every good and perfect gift is from above, coming down from the Father of the heavenly lights, who does not change like shifting shadows."
   >
   > *James 1:16-17*

3. Consider the amazing gifts of salvation that God has given to you through Christ: He has freely given you forgiveness of your sins. You will escape the eternal wrath of Hell. You can experience His love today. Allow your heart to overflow with thankfulness.

4. Move throughout your home, continually giving thanks for all that you see. Go throughout your kitchen, fridge, and pantry and thank God for all of the food that He has given you.

5. Now take time to thank God for your children and spouse and friends. Thank Him for their love for you and each other.

6. Now move outside your home and focus upon God's creation. Thank Him for all that you see. Take your time with this.

7. Now move back into your home. Look within a mirror and thank God for making you. Allow Him to speak to you concerning the amazing gift that you are to this world and His Kingdom.

8. Now find a quiet spot and allow the Holy Spirit to open your eyes more to the amazing reality of your Heavenly Provider.

The Discipline of Memorization:

1 Thessalonians 5:18

> "...give thanks in all circumstances, for this is God's will for you in Christ Jesus."

Philippians 2:14

> "Do everything without complaining or arguing..."

The Discipline of Prayer:

Dear Heavenly Provider, You are so good and kind and generous. You always provide for me in abundance. I thank you Father for all of your amazing gifts. You give me good food, good friends, and so much more (take your time to thank Him for as much as you can think of). I confess my tremendous shortcoming in failing to thank You always. Help me to give thanks in all things, so as to give you the glory that is rightfully Yours.

Amen.

CHAPTER 4

PROTECTOR

> *"I will remain in the world no longer, but they are still in the world, and I am coming to you. Holy Father, <u>protect them</u> by the power of your name—the name you gave me—<u>so that they may be one</u> as we are one."*
>
> -- John 17:11

We live in a dangerous world. Despite the civilized atmosphere that our culture tries to surround itself with, there is no escaping the physical, emotional, and spiritual peril that is lurking around every corner. Sickness, depression, sin, warfare, contempt, addiction, abuse, and idolatry are only a few of the land mines that have been buried within our daily context. No matter how hard we try to set our feet in such a way as to avoid these traps of the enemy, the outcome is inevitable: we will be victims of the darkness. Indeed, we are also doomed to be the culprits of such peril. The only hope to escape such evil is to run to our Protector. He alone is our cure from the dangers of the enemy.

As in all things, the world tries to take the place of the Living God by providing protection for us from these things. We run to relationships, media, medication, food, and other things, very often running into one form of darkness in order to escape another. All the solutions of this world are insufficient. They are based on a deceitful philosophy that often mimics God's Kingdom, but is far from being true protection and freedom.

From the beginning of human history, God has offered Himself to mankind as Protector. In the beginning He protected Adam and Eve through a clear warning concerning the Tree of the Knowledge of Good and Evil. Immediately following their sin, He protected Adam and Eve by removing them from the garden, away from the Tree of Life. All throughout the Bible, we see God protecting His children, at times through His mighty hand, and at other times through His chastisement (Hebrews 12:5-11). It is crucial that the disciple of Jesus sees God's chastisement as protection. Why do I discipline my children when they do wrong? It's to protect them from doing it again. It's to help them stay away from the thinking of this world which leads to death. God is our Father. And as a good Father He will not be silent when we choose to engage in the activity of the enemy. Your Father will fight for you. He is your protector and hiding place.

> "You are my hiding place; you will protect me from trouble and surround me with songs of deliverance. Selah"
>
> Psalm 32:7

The word 'Selah' refers to a pause so that you can meditate on the truth given. What does it mean to immerse yourself in your Protector? It means to hide yourself in Him. It is to open the ears of your heart so that you might hear His songs of deliverance. How often do we, when troubled, run and hide in the thinking, sins, and addictions of this world? This is to immerse ourselves in the world, and the result is always the same; we are left emptier and in more pain than before. Jesus, however, is inviting us to partake in our original purpose. And in order to do that, we must be immersed in Him as our Protector.

The practical application of this reality is quite simple, yet extremely powerful. How do we immerse ourselves in God's protection? Simply put, *we stay away from sin*.

> "If you obey my commands, you will remain in my love..."
>
> John 15:10

Scripture tells us that the wages of sin is death. Human history has validated this claim. Consider the danger and pain and destruction that this world has experienced. Can it not all be traced back to sin? The point is simple: ***The moment you choose to sin, you step out from under the protection of your King and into the camp of the enemy.*** (Read this point again.) God, of course, can still reach you there, but in His sovereignty He has given you free will. And with your free will, you can choose to bring immense harm to yourself and others through sin.

The safest place that you can be is within the will of God, living a life of love for God and others. We tend to not see this. Most of us feel safer in the comfort of our home while engaging in sin than we do in a rough neighborhood while walking in obedience. We must allow God to open our eyes to the invisible realities concerning the consequences of sin. If you are currently outside of the strong walls of God, then I would advise you to repent of whatever sin has entangled you and to run into the protecting arms of your Heavenly Dad.

Another important principle regarding our Protector is that of *fear*. This world thrives on fear, and yet, within the arms of our Abba there is no need for fear to be present. We don't have to fear the things this world fears such as disaster, death, and the opinions of others. Neither do we have to fear the darkness that is around us. If we are outside of our Protector, then yes, we should be afraid, but within His hands we are well protected.

> "My sheep listen to my voice; I know them, and they follow me. I give them eternal life, and they shall never perish; no one can snatch them out of my hand."
>
> *John 10:27,28*

According to this verse, who is safe in God's hand? It is his sheep (those who listen to His voice and follow Him). This is what it means to immerse yourself in your Protector. It means to immerse yourself in Him through obedience. It means to see Him as the only true shelter from the storms of this world. Within Him, there is no need to fear the darkness.

> "For God hath not given us the spirit of fear; but of power, and of love, and of a sound mind."
>
> *2 Timothy 1:7 (KJV)*

THE EXAMPLE OF JESUS

Was Jesus ever in danger? From one perspective, yes. He continually had people out to kill Him. He was a target for many, from thieves to kings. As He wandered the desert for forty days he could have been overcome by starvation or some wild animal. And yet, was Jesus ever in real danger? Not from His perspective. He was always safe. Why? Because His Father was His hiding place. Jesus continually immersed Himself in the reality that His Abba was mighty to save. Fear, was never an option. Even in death, Jesus was safe. Think about that. Even at the hands of the Romans; even under the condemnation of the religious authorities, Jesus was completely protected. Why? Because He had an Abba who was all powerful, and desired for His Son to die. Jesus submerged Himself into the reality that no one could touch Him without the will of His Father. Jesus was also very careful to walk in complete obedience to His Father, so as to never stray outside of His protection. This should likewise be our attitude, knowing that we need not fear the terror of this world, but only God who is King.

THE EXAMPLE OF DAVID

We see both good and poor examples to follow in the life of King David. When he chose to obey and honor God, he was safe and secure. He enjoyed blessing and joy and inner peace. And yet, when he chose to stray from his Father's will, he became an adulterer and a murderer. He did not stay immersed within His protector. He is a wonderful example for us that the consequences concerning whether or not we remain in our Father's protection are enormous, whether good or bad.

THE CHALLENGE

The challenge and instruction is simple: ***Say no to sin and obey God***. Much of the church today, however, has bought into the lie-based thinking that living a life characterized by obedience is nearly impossible. This philosophy is not only wrong, but also leads us outside of our Protector. As God's children we are to be in the world, but not of the world. As it says in Scripture:

> "Do not be yoked together with unbelievers. For what do righteousness and wickedness have in common? Or what fellowship can light have with darkness? [15] What

> harmony is there between Christ and Belial? What does a believer have in common with an unbeliever?"
>
> *2 Corinthians 5:14-15*

The point here is simple: we should not look like this world. We should not be involved in the sinful activity and mindset of this world. The reason for this is explained in the following verses:

> "<u>For we are the temple of the living God</u>. As God has said: "I will live with them and walk among them, and I will be their God, and they will be my people." "Therefore come out from them and be separate, says the Lord. Touch no unclean thing, and I will receive you." "I will be a Father to you, and you will be my sons and daughters, says the Lord Almighty."
>
> *2 Corinthians 5:16-18*

Did you know that you are the temple of God? God lives in you through His Spirit, and therefore desires you to **come out and be separate** and to **touch no unclean thing**. This is what it means to be His children and for Him to be your Father. The conclusion for us is given in the following verse, and herein lies our challenge:

> "Since we have these promises, dear friends, let us purify ourselves from everything that contaminates body and spirit, perfecting holiness out of reverence for God."
>
> *2 Corinthians 7:1*

God has given us a wonderful promise: as we separate ourselves from this world (not geographically, but rather in the area of activity and thinking) we will experience the father-child relationship for which we were made. Therefore, what should our reaction be? We should ***purify ourselves from everything that contaminates body and spirit***. What a sad thing it is for the born-again Christian to contaminate the temple of God through sin and worldliness! According to this verse, we don't have to! We can purify ourselves from the darkness of this world! This is the challenge our Protector has put before us. God wants you to immerse yourself in Him as you ***perfect holiness out of reverence for God***.

It is time for us to be purposeful and responsible regarding the state of our body and spirit. You have a Protector available to you 24/7. The more you get away from sin and into Him, the more you will experience His Kingdom. The choice is yours.

END NOTES:

Main Points:

- God is the perfect protection from darkness, sin, and death.
- We immerse ourselves in Him by obeying Him.

Questions to Consider:

- How much of your life is lived within the protecting arms of your Abba? How much outside?
- What specific sins or ways of thinking or attitudes are keeping you outside of God's protection?
- What things of this world do you run to for protection or coping when you feel afraid?

The Discipline of Study:

Read 2 Timothy 2:22. What insight does this verse give you regarding the idea of God's protection?

Read Ephesians 5:3-7. What insights does this passage give you? What aspects of the church's thinking (or your thinking) are challenged by this passage?

Look up John 15:4 and 1 Corinthians 15:34. What insight do these passages give you? What phrase do they both share?

The Discipline of Meditation:

Imagine yourself in a barren wasteland. There is no water. Nothing green lives there. And everywhere there are wolves, hyenas, and lions hunting you. You manage to fight them off for the most part, yet the encounters have left you beaten and bruised and in need of medical attention. Many other people are wandering the same desert, with the same wounds, and many lay dead on the ground. Just when you think all hope is lost you find a castle. Within the castle is everything you had ever hoped for; food, drink, safety, and rest. There are others there. They are safe within the walls. Yet from time to time, some will venture outside of the fortress. Often they return, tattered and torn. Other times they never come back, their corpses remaining torn apart on the desert floor. Take some time to meditate upon the darkness and death that surrounds you in the real world. Thank God for His refuge and protection that He offers. Take time to confess any sin in your life, and do whatever is necessary to separate yourself from it, as is appropriate. Now take some time to meditate on Proverbs 18:10.

The Discipline of Memorization:

Psalm 97:10

> "Let those who love the Lord hate evil, for he guards the lives of his faithful ones and delivers them from the hand of the wicked."

Psalm 32:7

> "You are my hiding place; you will protect me from trouble and surround me with songs of deliverance. Selah"

Proverbs 18:10

> "The name of the LORD is a strong tower; the righteous run to it and are safe."

The Discipline of Prayer:

Dear Father, thank You for protecting me, even sometimes when I don't deserve it. Thank you also for allowing me at times to be beat up by the enemy because it shows me my need for You. Open my eyes Lord, that I might run within the walls of You so that I might find rest and peace. Work in me a hatred for sin and a love for light. Thank You for being You, my strong fortress.

Amen!

CHAPTER 5

CREATOR

"Creation is the primary and most perfect revelation of the Divine."

-- Thomas Aquinas

We will at this point transition from the Father to the Son. The New Testament does not leave any doubt that those whom Christ has chosen are now ***in Him***. This is something true of all disciples, and yet, there is still a responsibility left to each of us to practically immerse ourselves more and more in Lord Jesus Christ. As we know Christ more, we will be able to immerse ourselves in Him in a way that will radically transform our lives. We will know Him and the amazing truths of His Kingdom. However, knowledge by itself is not enough. In addition to hearing these realities, we must also do them. Application is what is lacking in the church today. Let us therefore endeavor not only to understand these things, but to also put them into practice.

Let us now consider what it means to immerse ourselves in the person of Christ. When it comes to Jesus, most of us focus solely upon His work on the cross. This work, of course, is beautiful. We are forgiven through the blood of our King. Many of us, however, stop our immersion process here, not because we are not open for more of God, but simply because we haven't given thought to the fact that there is more to experience beyond forgiveness.

> "We have not received the spirit of the world but the Spirit who is from God, that we may understand what God has freely given us."
>
> *1 Corinthians 2:12*

What has God freely given us? To put it simply, Himself. And with Him comes endless opportunities of experiencing His character, power, and love. There are so many different ways to immerse ourselves into the person and activity of Jesus Christ that it can be difficult to know where to begin. The question we need to ask is, **When in the scriptures do we first see Jesus at work?** The answer concerns creation.

> "For by him all things were created: things in heaven and on earth, visible and invisible, whether thrones or powers or rulers or authorities; all things were created by him and for him."
>
> *Colossians 1:16*

How do you immerse yourself in Jesus the Creator? This is a life-changing question. Let us answer it by asking another question. How would you immerse yourself in the person of Michelangelo? Would you not seek out the Sistine Chapel? You would walk its halls and look intently upon its every detail. Likewise, if you wanted to immerse yourself in the person of Beethoven you would listen to Symphony 9, the whole time considering the man behind the music. You would do likewise with any writer, artist, baker, or builder that you wanted to know. Do you not realize what our God has given us? He has given us an art gallery, ranging from the enormous stars and mountains and nebulas all the way down to the most microscopic elements of life. He has given us a continual concerto of song and sound, from the cooing of a newborn baby to the trumpet call of the mighty elephant to the sonnet of leaves in the wind. He has given us infinite fragrances and tastes which never grow dull, from the rose to the lime to a gentle kiss. Everywhere we go we see it and sense it. It is ever with us. We are trapped (in a good way) in the gallery of our King. We can never escape it for the simple reason that we can never escape ourselves, we who are the chief of all of God's creations. How sad it would be to walk through the Sistine Chapel and never once consider the one who adorned it. Likewise, how sad it is to consider the fact that we are continually shown the mind of our Lord through creation, and yet often fail to recognize it.

> "The heavens declare the glory of God; the skies proclaim the work of his hands. Day after day they pour forth speech; night after night they display knowledge. There is no speech or language where their voice is not heard. Their voice goes out into all the earth, their words to the ends of the world."
>
> *Psalms 19:1-4*

Let us take our analogy of Michelangelo a step further. Let us say that as you walked through the Sistine Chapel, that you did so not only knowing about Michelangelo, but actually knowing the man personally. Perhaps you were his child or spouse or dear friend. What emotions would surface during your tour of that chapel? It would be very meaningful. Every color and image would remind you of the personality, friendship, and love of your dear friend. Now, let's take it even another step further. Let's say that you not only knew Michelangelo personally, but that he was there with you as you walked within his creation.

How wonderful that would be! You would be able to tell him face to face how amazing of an artist and a man he is. Not only that, but he would likely explain to you why he did certain things the way he did them. Imagine doing that with your favorite artist, leader, or figure. This is what we are able to do every day with our Creator. As we walk the halls of creation, and as we look within the eyes of the people that He knit together, we are able to see His character and beauty, all the time praising Him for it. How many sunrises or sunsets have you seen in your life? I'm not talking about just seeing them in the process, but rather sitting down and watching from beginning to end the birth or end of the day? How many times have you done this while practicing the presence of your Creator? If you try this you will rightly find it to be more entertaining than any cinema and more romantic than any kiss. You will know your King better than before. Every disciple that is seeking to immerse themselves in their Creator would do well to own both a telescope and a microscope. To know (experientially) that the One who formed the rings of Saturn is the same One who gave sight to the blind is something God desires of us. To know that the One who created the bacteria that crawls within a single drop of water is to also know the One who shed His blood on the cross.

A question that helps give all this perspective is, ***How often can I immerse myself in my Creator?*** The answer is, **continually**! And as you continually immerse yourself in His creation, your heart will overflow with worship. Just as seeing God as our Provider produces within us continual thanksgiving, so also recognizing Him as Creator produces within us continual praise. What if your earthly father made the universe? How often would you think of Him as you continually looked upon His handiwork? And most importantly, how would this practice affect your daily life? Immersing yourself in God doesn't just yield good conversations and biblical knowledge, but rather brings about true transformation and life. It makes us look more like our God, in whose image we were created. I believe that Jesus got up before the sunrise (Mark 1:35) not only to be alone, but also to look upon the stars and to watch the first gleams of the new day. This is also why Jesus would often ask His listeners to consider the creation, such as birds and lilies. He knew that within creation there is so much of God to be understood.

You and I stand without excuse when it comes to the question of whether Christ has revealed Himself to us or not.

> "For since the creation of the world God's invisible qualities—his eternal power and divine nature—have been clearly seen, being understood from what has been made, so that men are without excuse."
>
> Romans 1:20

We are within the colonnade of Christ's mind, and it is beautiful. You could spend your entire life searching out the beauty of the creation, and not only would you be unable to complete your quest, but you would also have lived a full life.

THE EXAMPLE OF PAUL

> "We went on ahead to the ship and sailed for Assos, where we were going to take Paul aboard. He had made this arrangement because he was going there on foot."
>
> Acts 20:13

Within this account, Paul separates himself from his companions and chooses to take the one day journey to Assos by foot instead of by boat. This is only presumption, but I believe that Paul was refueling his spirit through God's creation. He could have likewise done the same thing from the boat with his comrades, but there is something very important about getting alone with God and His creation. Getting alone with God in nature was a common practice for many people within the scriptures. They did this to immerse themselves in their Creator.

THE CHALLENGE

How sad it is for us to be bored with our surroundings. This is because of our blindness to Christ and His character. If your spouse, or parent, or best friend made the earth, you would never forget it. Everywhere you looked, you would see them through what they had made. This is what we must do concerning Christ and His creation. Everywhere we look, every sweet sound we hear, every pleasant smell and taste, every touch, these things should cause our hearts to overwhelm with praise for our Lord and King. The challenge before us is to stop failing to recognize Christ in His creation. We must turn away from the television to the real entertainment of creation. Likewise, when we are between our daily activities, we must not always look to our smart phone in order to fill the time, but should instead take in the surrounding artwork of our Savior. In doing so, we will continually be practicing the presence of our King and will adore Him everywhere we go.

END NOTES:

Main Points:

- Creation reveals God to us.
- Immersing ourselves in the creation will bring about a deeper adoration of God.
- Immersing ourselves in the creation will help us to practice God's presence.

Questions to Consider:

- What aspects of God's creation move your heart the most?
- What parts of God's creation do you encounter every day, yet fail to consider as God's handiwork and so move your heart to worship?
- Have you allowed yourself to worship God for how he made you? If not, what lies or other thoughts are keeping you from doing so?

The Discipline of Study:

Many men and angels began their prayers with a declaration that God made the heavens and the earth. (See Isaiah 37:16; Jeremiah 32:17; Acts 4:24; Revelation 14:7) Why do you think they did this? How does the understanding of Jesus being the Creator completely transform you understanding of the Christian life?

The Discipline of Meditation:

Watch either a sunrise or sunset. Try to watch it while practicing the presence of your Creator. (Do as if Jesus were physically sitting next to you.) You might want to do it in complete silence or with music. Allow your heart to overflow with majesty and wonder for your King. Now read aloud Psalm 148.

Go outside on a clear starlit night. Sit or lie down under the stars and allow them to minister to you. Meditate on the fact that the same Jesus who made you and died for you also made these amazing balls of light. Sing if you want to sing. Talk to Jesus and praise Him.

The Discipline of Memorization:

Amos 4:13

> "He who forms the mountains, creates the wind, and reveals his thoughts to man, he who turns dawn to darkness, and treads the high places of the earth— the LORD God Almighty is his name."

Psalms 19:1-4

> "The heavens declare the glory of God; the skies proclaim the work of his hands. Day after day they pour forth speech; night after night they display knowledge. There is no speech or language where their voice is not heard. Their voice goes out into all the earth, their words to the ends of the world."

The Discipline of Prayer:

O LORD Almighty, God of Israel, enthroned between the cherubim, You alone are God over all the kingdoms of the earth. You have made heaven and earth. Nothing is too hard for you. You made the earth by Your power; You founded the world by Your wisdom and stretched out the heavens by Your understanding. You who brings out the starry host one by one, and calls them each by name. Because of Your great power and mighty strength, not one of them is missing. Now, oh God, I give You thanks, and praise Your glorious name. I worship You! Amen.

CHAPTER 6

BROTHER

"Who, being in very nature God, did not consider equality with God something to be grasped, but made himself nothing, taking the very nature of a servant, being made in human likeness."

--Philippians 2:6-7

There are too many aspects of Jesus' character to rightly cover in this book. And again, the goal of this volume is not to give you every facet of God, but rather to set your feet on the path to knowing Him better. When it comes to the person of Christ, there is one characteristic that is overlooked more than any other and even denied by some. This is the humanity of Jesus. When we ask the question, **How did Jesus live a sinless life and do the miracles that He did?** we must never buy into the thinking that, **Well, He was God. He can do anything!** It is crucial in the life of the believer to understand that when Jesus walked this earth that He never played the God card. Instead, we must see that Jesus was able to do what He did because He was a man, like us, and allowed the Spirit of God to lead Him and empower Him.

> "...how God anointed Jesus of Nazareth with the Holy Spirit and power, and how he went around doing good and healing all who were under the power of the devil, <u>because God was with him</u>."
>
> Acts 10:38

Why was Jesus able to do these great things? Was it because He was God? No, but rather because **God was with Him**. Jesus lived His life as a man. He is therefore our Brother.

> "Both the one who makes men holy and those who are made holy are of the same family. So Jesus is not ashamed to call them brothers."
>
> Hebrews 2:11

Jesus calls us brothers because He became one of us. Understand also that this humanity of Jesus was not for only the thirty years that He walked this earth. When He chose to step into a human body roughly 2,000 years ago He did so for eternity. He will forever be human. This should encourage us in realizing how much God is committed to the human race!

Unfortunately, most Christians today see Jesus' life as nothing more than God being God. What I mean is, they don't see Jesus' life as very practical to their own. ***Jesus lived a life of godliness, power, and love. But big deal. He was God!*** This is the common perception, and therefore most of us have immersed ourselves in this thinking. And what is the result? We draw no daily encouragement from the life of Christ. Actually, if we are honest, all we draw from His life is discouragement. His life is just one big slap in the face of what we will never be able to possess this side of heaven.

Instead of immersing ourselves in this faulty way of thinking, we need to immerse ourselves in the reality that Jesus lived life as one of us. ***He is our Brother.*** What does that mean? ***It means that what He did, you can do.*** He even went on to say that we would do greater things than He did. The more that we wrap our heads around the fact the Jesus lived His life 100% as a man, the more we will be able to draw our encouragement and strength from our Brother Jesus Christ. Something important to understand is that Jesus wants us to know Him as our Brother. He wants to be a Brother to us.

> "Since the children have flesh and blood, he too shared in their humanity... For this reason he had to be made like his brothers in every way... Because he himself suffered when he was tempted, he is able to help those who are being tempted."
>
> Hebrews 2:14,17,18

According to this passage, why is Jesus able to help us when we are tempted? It is not because of His deity but rather His humanity. He can relate with our battle with darkness, temptation, doubt, and pride, for He was tempted as we are, yet was without sin.

Jesus is also our perfect example. He lived life as we should. He was baptized, anointed with the Holy Spirit, and led/empowered by the Holy Spirit.

> "As soon as Jesus was baptized, he went up out of the water. At that moment heaven was opened, and he saw the Spirit of God descending like a dove and lighting on him. And a voice from heaven said, "This is my Son, whom I love; with him I am well pleased." Then Jesus

> was led by the Spirit into the desert to be tempted by the devil."

> *Matthew 3:16-4:1*

Notice in this passage that Jesus was a man who was baptized, loved by God, and led by the Spirit. Does that sound familiar? It should sound familiar because it should be the experience of every disciple of Christ today. You can experience a life of victory through the leading and empowering of God's Holy Spirit. How do I know this? Because Jesus lived a life of victory through the leading and empowering of the Holy Spirit. Don't let this discourage you, but rather encourage and empower you that Jesus is the perfect example of what God will do with you if you let Him. This is what it means to immerse yourself in your Brother Jesus Christ.

THE EXAMPLE OF PETER

Peter's journey is so precious in that it demonstrates a man's growth from infancy to maturity. Peter, who was rebuked by Christ, abandoned Christ, and then denied Christ did not allow his discouragement to get the best of him. Instead, he allowed the human example of Jesus to be for him something possible to attain.

> "To this you were called, because Christ suffered for you, leaving you an example, that you should follow in his steps."

> *1 Peter 2:21*

Peter dared to believe that Jesus' example was something that we could follow. And in doing so, Peter led thousands to repentance, stood faithful in the face of torture, and eventually followed His Brother Jesus' example to the cross. He believed in Jesus' calling for Him to *feed my sheep*. He immersed himself in His Brother.

THE CHALLENGE

You can no longer buy into the thinking that Jesus' amazing life and example was simply Him being God. You must instead embrace the biblical truth that Jesus lived His life as one of us. Your attitude needs to be, **What Jesus did, I can do**. This is, after all, Jesus' attitude toward you:

> "I tell you the truth, anyone who has faith in me will do what I have been doing. He will do even greater things than these, because I am going to the Father."
>
> John 14:12

> "But just as he who called you is holy, so be holy in all you do; for it is written: "Be holy, because I am holy."
>
> 1 Peter 1:15,16

You and I are without excuse. If we choose to stand before Christ's throne one day with nothing good to show for the life we lived, it will not be because God didn't give us what we needed. Instead, it will be because we didn't take hold of it.

END NOTES:

Main Points:

- Jesus never played the God card.
- Jesus lived His life 100% as a man.
- What Jesus did, I can do.

Questions to Consider:

- Up until now, how had you viewed the example of Christ in relationship to your own life?
- How does it encourage you that Jesus lived His life as a man?
- What sinful practice/attitude do you currently possess that this chapter encourages you to get rid of because of Jesus' example?

The Discipline of Study:

We often think of all that Jesus did as being impossible for mortal man to accomplish. Beside each characteristic or deed of Jesus that is listed below, see if you can think of other people in the Bible that did the same thing.

- Walked on water
- Raised the dead
- Arose from the dead
- Healed people by letting the sick touch their clothing
- Healed people with their shadow
- Change the weather
- Opened the eyes of the blind

- Multiplied food
- Healed the lame
- Rebuked evil spirits
- Ascended into heaven

How does this study encourage you regarding your potential as a son of God?

The Discipline of Meditation:

Consider Jesus in the garden on the night He was betrayed. Feel the anxiety that was so heavy upon His heart. Try to imagine the intensity with which three times Jesus asked His Father to not make Him go to the cross. Picture yourself there praying with Jesus. Imagine with heartache and sadness. Then consider how, as a man, Jesus resolved to follow through with the will of His Father. Ask God to give you, as a man, the same passion for obedience to your Father. Then read Philippians 2:5-11. Meditate on the humility and obedience of Christ.

The Discipline of Memorization:

John 14:12

> "I tell you the truth, anyone who has faith in me will do what I have been doing. He will do even greater things than these, because I am going to the Father."

1 Peter 2:21

> "To this you were called, because Christ suffered for you, leaving you an example, that you should follow in his steps."

The Discipline of Prayer:

Dear Brother Jesus,

Thank You for humbling Yourself and becoming one of us. You have left me a perfect example of what it means to walk in Your Kingdom. May I not see Your example as a hindrance, but rather as an encouragement. May I live my life on this earth just as You did, in obedience to Your Father through the Holy Spirit. Amen.

CHAPTER 7

SAVIOR

> *"The next day John saw Jesus coming toward him and said, "Look, the Lamb of God, who takes away the sin of the world!"*
>
> *--John 1:29*

To say that Jesus' person and life are truly amazing is an understatement. He is the Creator; the great I Am. He is before all things, and yet, in a small village outside of Jerusalem He became one of us. And as a man, He saved us from all of our sins. In Book One of this series, Discipleship, we discuss briefly how Jesus saved us by His preaching, teaching, and work on the cross. The question that we will answer here deals with how we immerse ourselves, practically speaking, in Him as Savior. Scripture speaks very specifically about this, and it is all wrapped up with Jesus' death, burial, and resurrection. What we will discover is that Jesus has already put us into Himself, and that we therefore have everything we need to experience the benefits of this unity with our Savior.

Immersing ourselves in our Savior, according to scripture, is a three step process. It begins first with <u>knowing who we are</u>, or what is true of us. Once we are conscious of who we are, the next step is to <u>align our attitude with this reality</u>. Then, and only then, will we be able to <u>offer ourselves to God</u> in a way that results in a holy life. What I am saying here is not a manmade curriculum for life in God's Kingdom, but is instead taken right from the paper and ink of the sixth chapter of Romans. Let us now learn anew of who we are. Let us immerse ourselves in our Savior.

> "What shall we say, then? Shall we go on sinning so that grace may increase? By no means! We died to sin; how can we live in it any longer? Or don't you know that all of us who were baptized into Christ Jesus
>
> were baptized into his death?"
>
> Romans 6:1-3

Paul asks the question, **Shall we go on sinning so that grace may increase?** Clearly, there were people in those days who were answering this question with a definite *Yes*. And yet Paul's answer was an emphatic *No*. This again, is the good news of Jesus Christ. We don't have to go on sinning. We can be free from the reign of sin today.

Paul then teaches us something that is true of us. ***We died***. Did you know that? Did you know that you died? When you were put into Jesus, you were also put into His death. Just as Jesus died you also died. What does that mean? It means that you died to the power of sin. You no longer have to obey sin as your master. You're dead to it. Whether you know it or not, if you are a disciple, this is true of you. You have been set free from sin and have become slaves to righteousness.

I think a tremendous analogy of this is the abolition of slavery around the world during the nineteenth century. Many countries within Europe, for example, were declaring all slaves free. Something interesting to note is that it in many instances, it took months for this news to reach the ears of the slaves. This meant that these people were free, even though they didn't know it. They thought they were still slaves, yet legally, they weren't. This meant that you had free people, with no legal hold binding them, living as slaves when they didn't need to. The only thing holding them back was a lack of knowledge. They didn't know the good news of their freedom.

Many of us, likewise have been living as if we were slaves to sin when all of this time, as Christians, we have been freed men. Jesus' work on the cross was His good news of freedom to all who would follow Him. On the day we were born again we were therefore set free from sin. We no longer have to do it. It is no longer our master. For some of us reading this, today might be our good news of freedom from slavery. Today might be the day when we learn that all of this time we were set free from sin, and are therefore able to live righteously.

Not only did we die with Christ, but we were also buried with Him and risen with Him.

> "We were therefore buried with him through baptism into death in order that, just as Christ was raised from the dead through the glory of the Father, we too may live a new life. If we have been united with him like this in his death, we will certainly also be united with him in his resurrection."
>
> Romans 6:4-5

What does it mean to be buried with Him? It means that Christ didn't just take who we were before we knew Him and make us better. He completely started over. Your 'old man' was put to death and buried. And there in the ground it remains. Jesus isn't interested in making corrupted mankind better. What He is interested in is a new creation. And that is what we are in Him. **...*just as Christ was raised from the dead through the glory of the Father, we too may live a new life*.** You have been raised with Christ. Your old self remains buried while you are risen to life as a new creation. This is the concept that both Jesus and Peter referred to as being ***born again***. The old you, the slave to sin, has been done away with. You are now a new creation, and you are free.

This is the first step in immersing ourselves in our Savior. We must know ourselves. We must know who we are. Without the news of their freedom, the free men and women and children would have continued to live like slaves. **Likewise, if we do not rightly understand who we are in Christ, it will be impossible to live the way that God wants us to live.** Unless we know that we are free, we will live as slaves to Satan and his kingdom.

As previously stated, the first step in immersing ourselves in our Savior is to know ourselves. The process however does not end here. Let us consider again the slaves around the world who gained their freedom. If they were going to experience their liberty, they couldn't simply know that they were free. They had to believe it. They had to walk in it. They had to have an attitude that lived in accordance to this wonderful news. I am sure that there were many people who continued to live as slaves simply because they could not accept the message of their freedom. It was too foreign to their experience, or it was too good to be true. I'm sure for others their initial reaction that next morning was to go out to work as slaves because this was their habit. And yet many of them probably stopped in their tracks, and laughing to themselves, said, ***Wait a minute. I'm not a slave. I'm free.*** And turning away from their former masters, they ventured on to freedom. Paul tells us to do the same thing. He teaches us that we must have an attitude that lives in light of the fact that we have died to sin and have been born again. Look at what he says:

> "The death he (Jesus) died, he died to sin once for all; but the life he lives, he lives to God.
>
> In the same way, <u>count yourselves</u> dead to sin but alive to God in Christ Jesus."
>
> *Romans 6:10-11*

Once again, Paul likens us to Jesus. Jesus died to sin and now lives unto God. ***In the same way***, we are to count ourselves dead to sin and alive to God. The word here translated ***count*** means to regard or reckon something as true. We are to regard ourselves as that which God says; people who are dead to sin and alive to God. It is important to note that this second step is something that you must do. It won't be done for you. You are to live in light of the fact that you have been identified with the death, burial, and resurrection of Jesus Christ. You are to make this your attitude. Attitude is important. Most Christians wake up daily with an attitude that is very worldly. It tells us to walk after the things of this world. It also tells us that living a victorious life in Christ is virtually impossible. But as we immerse ourselves in Jesus, our attitude will change. We will wake up in the morning with a mind-set that is focused on Jesus and His Kingdom. We will see ourselves as someone who is perfectly able to say *no* to sin.

Something we must understand is that our attitude will automatically determine our experience. If a professional swimmer approaches the starting block with an attitude that says, *I'm not going to win*, then they will undoubtedly get that which they expected. If your outlook on life is that you are always going to struggle with and give in to sin then you have already determined how you will finish the race of life. You will fail. This is the mental reality that Paul is here addressing in Romans. If we are going to experience freedom from sin then we must begin with an attitude that matches. Fortunately, Jesus has given us everything we need in Himself to have an attitude of victory. I'm sure that the ex-slaves around the world underwent the same mental exercise. They had to wake up and go throughout their day with the attitude, *I'm no longer a slave. I am free.* Without this, they would've ended up back on the plantations living like slaves. I'm sure for many, this unfortunately took place. They chose to live a lie because they couldn't believe and accept what was true of them. And this still happens today in the context of Christians who choose to live like slaves of the enemy because their attitude is not aligned with God's Kingdom. Once again, attitude is important. It makes us able to live lives of holiness. It makes us able to offer ourselves to God in a way that is pleasing to Him.

> "Therefore do not let sin reign in your mortal body so that you obey its evil desires. Do not offer the parts of your body to sin, as instruments of wickedness, but rather offer yourselves to God, as those who have been brought from death to life; and offer the parts of your body to him as instruments of righteousness."
>
> Romans 6:12-13

Therefore (since you are dead to sin and alive to Christ) do not let sin reign in your body, and do not offer yourselves to sin, but rather to God. This is the third step of immersing ourselves in our Savior. We offer ourselves to Him. We must recognize the necessary order of these steps. We cannot do this third step until we have done steps one and two. We must first know who we are, and then we must believe it to be true, therefore changing our attitudes. Then, and only then, will we be able to offer ourselves to God.

The above scripture refers to the parts of our body as instruments. The Greek word translated ***instrument*** is everywhere else in the New Testament translated ***weapon*** or ***armor*** (John 8:13, Romans 13:12, 2 Corinthians 6:7; 10:4). The parts of your body can either be offered as weapons for the enemy or offered as weapons for the cause of Christ. It's up to you. How do you offer them to

Christ? You must first know who you are. Then you must put on an attitude which agrees with who you are. Then you will be ready to fight the fight of love and holiness. As your Savior commands you to act, you will gladly obey, therefore making the parts of your body instruments of His Kingdom. This is what God wants. He wants you to be immersed in Him as our Savior. In His grace He has given you everything you need to do so. The choice remains yours.

THE EXAMPLE OF ME

Using myself as an example may at first seem very self-serving and/or conceited. But it is rather a testimony of what immersion in Jesus can do for even a sinful wretch like me. By the grace of God, I have experienced more character transformation in the past four years than I had in the previous 15, due primarily to the applications of the principles that I have here discussed. Not that I have by any means arrived at perfection (very far from that), but I have been able to experience freedom in certain areas that I had once considered impossible to be free from. You must understand me clearly; I am not free in the sense that it is impossible to sin, but rather I am free in the sense that I can now choose to act righteously, and by His grace, will often do so. If God can transform a person like me, sinful as I am, He can surely do the same for you. This is the power that comes with immersing ourselves in Jesus as our Savior.

THE CHALLENGE

There is an attitude in the church today that says that we will always be tied up and characterized by sin. You must cast this thinking away from yourself. You are able, through your Savior, to be free! The church has tried to replace character transformation with behavior modification. We try to teach people to be kind without any immersion in Christ. God is not impressed with behavior that opposes the nature of our hearts. He wants His love to flow through us from the inside out. Consequently, you will never transform anyone from the outside in. Transformation in God's Kingdom is always from the inside out. This comes through the immersion I have previously discussed.

> "Make a tree good and its fruit will be good…"
>
> Matthew 12:33

God wants your attitude to be, ***Sin has no power over me. I am instead a slave of God's righteousness***. ***I don't have to sin.*** If your attitude is anything short of this, then it will be virtually impossible to live the life that God desires for you.

> "You have been set free from sin and have become slaves to righteousness."
>
> Romans 6:18

END NOTES:

Main Points:

- You must know who you are (someone identified with Jesus' death, burial, and resurrection).
- You must regard yourself as dead to sin and alive to God.
- You must offer yourself to God.

Questions to Consider:

- Did you know that you are free from the power of sin?
- Does your attitude match up to the reality that you are dead to sin and alive to God? How so?
- How should this revelation transform your life?

The Discipline of Study:

Open your Bible to Romans 6. Begin by reading verses 1-14. This is what we discussed in this lesson. Now read the rest of the chapter. Take some time to record any observations/questions you might have. Then answer the questions below:

- According to verses 15-18, are you able to live a life of sin and offer yourselves to God at the same time? Do your actions, or your professed faith, determine who you are a slave to?
- Paul says that their 'obedience to a certain teaching' was what made them a slave to righteousness. Does this phrase challenge your thinking? What teaching do you think Paul was specifically referring to?

- According to the rest of the chapter, what is the benefit and result of being a slave of God?

The Discipline of Meditation:

Picture yourself as a slave on a plantation. Except this plantation is Satan's kingdom and your master is sin. Picture yourself working under the burden of sin. Then allow the Spirit to inform you of the freedom He has given you in Christ. Picture yourself free from all whips and chains. Imagine yourself walking off of the plantation and living a life of freedom. Now consider the memorization verse below. Read it slowly, except make it first person. *'I have been set free from sin and have become a slave to righteousness.'* Say it as many times as you can, and it still be personal and heart felt. Allow the Spirit to minister to you.

The Discipline of Memorization:

Romans 6:18

> "You have been set free from sin and have become slaves to righteousness."

The Discipline of Prayer:

Dear Heavenly Father, I thank You that you sent your Son to be my Passover Lamb. By Your great mercy, even when I was dead in my sins, You saved me. By your grace You placed me into Your Son, so that I might also be Your son, and likewise reign with You in this life and the life to come. Thank You so much. May I live my life as one who is dead to sin and alive to You. Amen.

CHAPTER 8

KING

""Jesus said, "My kingdom is not of this world. If it were, my servants would fight to prevent my arrest by the Jews. But now my kingdom is from another place." "You are a king, then!" said Pilate. Jesus answered, "You are right in saying I am a king. In fact, for this reason I was born, and for this I came into the world, to testify to the truth. Everyone on the side of truth listens to me.""

--John 18:36-37

Every kingdom must by definition have a king. Our King is Jesus Christ. His initial crown of thorns has been replaced with a crown of glory and He reigns over all. He has been given authority over both the heavens and the earth. Though He once emptied Himself of His divine power He has now reclaimed it. Though He is still humble of heart He is not humble to the eyes. Listen to John's portrayal of Him:

> "On the Lord's Day I was in the Spirit, and I heard behind me a loud voice like a trumpet... I turned around to see the voice that was speaking to me. And when I turned I saw seven golden lampstands, and among the lampstands was someone "like a son of man," dressed in a robe reaching down to his feet and with a golden sash around his chest. His head and hair were white like wool, as white as snow, and his eyes were like blazing fire. His feet were like bronze glowing in a furnace, and his voice was like the sound of rushing waters. In his right hand he held seven stars, and out of his mouth came a sharp double-edged sword. His face was like the sun shining in all its brilliance. When I saw him, I fell at his feet as though dead. Then he placed his right hand on me and said: "Do not be afraid. I am the First and the Last. I am the Living One; I was dead, and behold I am alive for ever and ever! And I hold the keys of death and Hades."
>
> *Revelation 1:10-18*

What a description! Read it over again and try your best to picture what John saw. This is our King! When John saw Him, he fell down as though dead. What does that mean? It means that John was so overwhelmed with fear and majesty together at the sight of Jesus reigning in His glory that he passed out. It is important to remember that this is the same King who was raised by Mary and Joseph. He is the same King who gave sight to the blind, was led by the Spirit, and who fed the hungry. He is Jesus; the same Jesus who prayed for you and me in the garden on the night of His betrayal. This is your King Jesus, and He desires with all of His heart that you immerse yourself in Him as your King.

What does it mean to immerse ourselves in Jesus our King? To answer this question we need to be educated in kings and kingdoms. In our current culture, kings and kingdoms are virtually void. A kingdom principle that we must therefore understand is that a king owns everything and everyone in his kingdom.

> "You are not your own; you were bought at a price."
>
> 1 Corinthians 6

Jesus owns you. Not only does He own you, but your family and possessions as well. If you want to use the terminology we discussed in Book One, Jesus owns your kingdom. This is why you are a steward. He has entrusted to you His possessions. (This thinking is completely contrary to the thinking of this world which says that I am my own master.) To immerse ourselves in our King is to first realize that we belong to Him. He is our King. He is our Lord. We are His servants. We are His sons. This means that if He desires something from us, we have no option concerning how we respond. We obey our King! Unfortunately, in the church today, obedience has become optional. What I mean is, we come before God's throne to seek His will, and once He makes it clear to us we think to ourselves, "Now that I know God's will, I need to think about what to do." We consider our response, instead of simply trusting and obeying our King. Trust and obey; this is the attitude of a servant of King Jesus.

In order to understand this specific immersion we must also consider kingdoms. What characterizes a kingdom? First, ***every kingdom has a culture.*** In our nation, we are democratic by nature. This means that the people rule the nation. The majority rules. This is not at all the culture of God's Kingdom. If all of the citizens of a kingdom agree that something should be done, and yet the king of that kingdom decides something different, then the king gets his way! You can surround yourself with the smartest people in the world (or even the smartest people in the church) so that they can tell you whatever you want to hear, and yet if it doesn't agree with the will and truth of our King Jesus, then it shouldn't be an option. What happens, unfortunately, is that when we become citizens of God's Kingdom, we try to walk in it according to the culture of our earthly nations. This doesn't work. **To immerse ourselves in our King is to live according to the culture of His Kingdom!** This is what it means to be in the world, but not of the world. We all know this saying, and yet we live like this world lives. We conform to its pattern of thinking. Do you know what the culture of God's Kingdom is like? Jesus described it to us in His teaching. In God's culture, to give is better than to receive; if someone curses, we bless; we store up our treasures in heaven; we give without expecting any return. This is how citizens of God's Kingdom act.

Another principle of a kingdom is that every good citizen and administrator of a kingdom functions by the authority of the king. They don't tell someone to open a door in their own name and authority, but instead say, 'Open in the name of the king!' Likewise, you are to immerse yourself in your King by doing *everything in His name.*

> "And whatever you do, whether in word or deed, do it all in the name of the Lord Jesus, giving thanks to God the Father through him."
>
> Colossians 3:17

We will not be able to rightly follow our King unless we do everything in His name. This is why so many of us experience continual frustration. We set out to do the works of our King and then experience both confusion and defeat because we don't understand how to act in Jesus' name. What does it mean to do everything in His name? First, it means to do them with Him. Remember, this is the same God into whom we are immersing ourselves as our Abba, our Provider, our Protector, our Creator, our Brother, and our Savior. We are therefore doing life with Him. When we go to say or do something we do not step out of His presence to do so. Instead, we do it with Him. Since before time began, God has always intended man to act with Him. This is why He made us like Him.

To act in His name also means that we do it in His strength and for His glory. Everything is about Him. As I love my family in the name of Jesus, I love them with His strength, and by His grace, and for His glory. I am doing everything I do in the authority of Jesus. This is what people implied when they would do battles or acts of kindness or whatever else they did in the name of Caesar. If a diplomat offered gifts to a foreign king in the name of Caesar, it was as if Caesar himself were delivering that gift. Caesar therefore received the thanksgiving and honor. The only reason that the diplomat was even able to do this good work was because of the authority given to him by Caesar. This is likewise what our situation is with our King Jesus Christ. We do His deeds of goodness through Him and by His authority.

> "For we are God's workmanship, created in Christ Jesus to do good works, which God prepared in advance for us to do."
>
> Ephesians 2:10

In order to experience the fullness of Jesus Christ we must live according to the reality that He is Lord. If Jesus is Lord, then allegiance and obedience are not items to leave unattended. We must live accordingly.

> "if you confess with your mouth, "Jesus is Lord," and believe in your heart that God raised him from the dead, you will be saved."
>
> Romans 10:9

To confess is to agree with. Anyone can say that the words *Jesus is Lord*. But simply saying these words isn't enough. This is why Jesus asked the logical question **Why do you call me Lord and don't do what I say?** If Jesus is your King, you will do what He says. This is what it means to immerse yourself in Him as King.

THE EXAMPLE OF 'THE HEROES'

Hebrews 11 gives us a wonderful list of men and women who obeyed God as their King. They obeyed without understanding. They gladly let the world take what they wanted to take, because they knew that their King owned everything. They became subject even to the point of death (which shouldn't surprise us since that is the example their King gave them). According to their King, the world was not worthy of them. They were heroes of God's Kingdom. This is what it means to be a disciple of Jesus who walks in obedience to his King. It is to not follow this world, but our King alone.

> "Instead, they were longing for a better country—a heavenly one. Therefore God is not ashamed to be called their God, for he has prepared a city for them."
>
> *Hebrews 11:16*

THE CHALLENGE

We live in a culture that is completely against Jesus being our King. More and more they want the government to be their king, and at the same time they want to be their own king. Jesus is not even an option in their thinking. Unfortunately, the church today has bought into this to the point that we likewise turn to the government and ourselves as our authority. In order to be a true disciple of Jesus, this point must be settled once and for all. Jesus is our King, therefore we follow Him, period! If the world tells us not to pray, then we disobey the world. If the world tells us not to share Christ in certain contexts, and in that context Jesus puts it on our heart to share His word, then we speak! We do not fear the consequences of this world because we know that our King is also our provider and He will take care of us. A disciple of Christ would rather suffer and/or die for the cause of his King than live in safety and comfort for the cause of this world. We must stop trying to justify away this principle. Jesus is your King, therefore, obey Him!

END NOTES:

Main Points:

- You immerse yourselves in your King by first realizing that you belong to Him.
- A King has absolute authority in His Kingdom!
- You immerse yourselves in your King by living according to the culture of His Kingdom.
- You immerse yourself in your King by doing everything in His name.
- True followers obey their King.

Questions to Consider:

- In what ways does your life reflect the fact that you belong to the Lord? In what ways does it not?
- How does your American culture transfer over to your walk with Christ? Think of specific examples.
- Jesus said, "Why do you call me 'Lord', but don't do what I say". How does this verse minister, encourage, or convict your experience as a Christian?

The Discipline of Study:

Read Revelation 19:11-21. When you read this, focus on the fact that this is speaking about your Holy King Jesus. Make a list of kingly characteristics from this passage that point to the activity of Jesus being our King. (For example, in verse 11 Jesus judges and makes war. These are both characteristics of a King). Record any additional observations/questions. How does this account challenge (or confirm) your view of Jesus?

The Discipline of Meditation:

Read Psalm 2. This is a prophecy of the Christ King. Begin by meditating on verses 1-6. Jesus is the ultimate authority. Any idea of this world overpowering Him brings laughter to Him and His Kingdom. Recite these verses two or three times nice and slowly and allow the Spirit to open your eyes up to these realities. Then read verses 7-9 a few times, slowly and humbly. Meditate on the fact that Jesus' has inherited the nations and that He will rule them with an iron scepter (Revelation 19:15).

Then read the rest of the Psalm and remember that you are a king of the earth, and that because this prophecy is true, that you should do what these verses say. Allow the Spirit to make this all very clear to you.

The Discipline of Memorization:

Colossians 3:17

> "And whatever you do, whether in word or deed, do it all in the name of the Lord Jesus, giving thanks to God the Father through him."

The Discipline of Prayer:

King Jesus, You are Lord over all of creation. You rule with majesty, honor, justice, and truth. One day every knee will bow and all of creation will confess that you are indeed King over all. To You, and You alone, be all glory and honor. I bow my knee, and I humbly confess, that You are King. Amen!

CHAPTER 9

JUDGE

"Moreover, the Father judges no one, but has entrusted all judgment to the Son…"

-- John 5:22

"For we know him who said, "It is mine to avenge; I will repay," and again, "The Lord will judge his people." It is a dreadful thing to fall into the hands of the living God."

--Hebrews 10:30-31

This characteristic of Christ is very often ignored or justified away. I think this is because the idea of being judged is not a happy one. No one welcomes judgment from another, much less from the One who knows everything about them! Others wrongly conclude that the Savior can't also be the Judge. Scripture tells us just the opposite. What we need to realize is that even though the idea of judgment is scary, it is something that when correctly understood will yield tremendous amounts of thanksgiving as well as a transformed life.

All of us stand before God as guilty criminals. We have broken His law by sinning against Him. This is understood by most people in the church today. What is also understood by many is the amazing revelation that by the blood of Jesus Christ we have been pardoned and set free from the consequences of our sin, and therefore, must no longer carry around the guilt of our iniquities. This is, as previously stated, our immersion in Jesus as Savior and Redeemer. He has redeemed us, or bought us back, from darkness and death. We are therefore free.

Unfortunately, our understanding seems to end here and we never take into account the reality that our Savior is also our Judge. What does this mean? It means that we will one day have to give an accounting of ourselves to Christ. Many people see this as opposed to grace. It is not. Scripture leaves no room for us to wiggle around this truth:

> "So we make it our goal to please him, whether we are at home in the body or away from it. For we must all appear before the judgment seat of Christ, that each one may receive what is due him for the things done while in the body, whether good or bad."
>
> 2 Corinthians 5:9,10

It says here that we **must all appear before the judgment seat of Christ**. It is inescapable. It is going to happen. We also read that we will receive our recompense for what we have done, **whether good or bad**.

This is why scripture tells us to fear God. We don't fear that He will suddenly hurt us because He is bored. Instead, we fear the idea of sinning against Him because He is Judge. This is what Christ spoke of in the Parable of the Talents found in Mathew 25. Each servant had to give an accounting of himself to his master, and each one was recompensed accordingly. This is the amazing opportunity we have. We can one day stand before Jesus and hear the words, ***Well done, good and faithful servant. Come and share in your Master's happiness!*** This is the greatest opportunity available to humanity.

What is your goal in life? I asked a group of young people this same question just recently. Ninety percent of their answers were either dealing with being wealthy or being a professional athlete. (A good reflection of our culture.) I gently communicated to them that compared to God's goal for their lives, their goals were lame. The goal of the disciple is to please Jesus Christ. ***So we make it our goal to please Him… 2 Corinthians 5:9.*** Why should this be our goal? Because He is the One to whom we must give an account. On that day, the only thing that will matter is whether or not we pleased Jesus.

Something we also observe in the Parable of the Talents is the consequence for a life void of pleasing the Judge.

> "And throw that worthless servant outside, into the darkness, where there will be weeping and gnashing of teeth."
>
> Matthew 25:30

This verse confuses many people today because they think it teaches that what we do saves us. Let me be very clear. We are saved by grace, through faith. The reality that Jesus is showing us here is that what we do reveals our faith. Jesus didn't forgive us so that we could do nothing. He forgave us so we could accomplish everything He commands. This servant had zero activity in the service of his master, and was therefore a man of zero faith. Jesus speaks of this connection between faith and action again in Matthew:

> "But I tell you that men will have to give account on the day of judgment for every careless word they have

spoken. For by your words you will be acquitted, and by your words you will be condemned."

Matthew 12:36,37

Jesus is NOT teaching here that we are justified by works. He just got finished explaining that what comes out of our mouths reveals who we are at the depths of our souls. Good trees bear good fruit. Bad trees bear bad fruit.

Let us now return to the point of this chapter. **Jesus is Judge.** Everyone will stand before Him to answer for the life they lived. What does this mean? It means that justice will be done! No one truly gets away with anything. We should be thankful for this. We should thank Jesus that He is Judge.

So what does it mean to walk in light of the fact that Jesus is Judge? It means to have the same priority that Paul had in the verse above, 2 Corinthians 5:9. It means that ***your primary goal in life will be to please God.*** Having goals is a good thing. What is your goal? Whatever it is, this one that Paul gives us is better. What would you rather have, all the treasure of this world, or hear the words ***well done*** at Jesus' throne? Which one of these is worth more? To immerse yourself in Jesus as your Judge is to live life through a completely different mindset than this world. Everything is not about today, but is rather about *that day*. Instead of asking the question, ***How will this decision affect my current situation or happiness***? we should rather be asking, ***How will this decision affect my standing before the judgment seat of Christ?***

Unfortunately, most of us don't live to please God, but rather live to please a spouse, parent, boss, or ourselves. This is because of a simple principle: We obey who we fear. If God wants you to do something, and your spouse wants you to do something different, who will you obey? ***You will obey the one that you fear the most.*** This is why seeing Jesus as our Judge is crucial to our level of obedience.

The fear of man lays a snare, but whoever trusts in the LORD is safe.

Proverbs 29:25

THE EXAMPLE OF JOB

"Then the Lord said to Satan, "Have you considered my servant Job? There is no one on earth like him; he is blameless and upright, a man who fears God and shuns evil."

Job 1:8

Job is often remembered for his hardships instead of his character. Job's life was indeed filled with tragedy, but immense blessing as well. Why was Job so blessed? Why did God esteem him as blameless and upright? Because He feared God and shunned evil (to do the first leads to the second). He understood that God would one day judge his life and he therefore acted appropriately.

"I made a covenant with my eyes not to look lustfully at a girl. For what is man's lot from God above, his heritage from the Almighty on high? Is it not ruin for the wicked, disaster for those who do wrong? Does he not see my ways and count my every step?"

Job 31:1-4

'The fear of the Lord—that is wisdom, and to shun evil is understanding.'

Job 28:28

THE CHALLENGE

You must start living your life as if you are going to end up before Christ as Judge. You will not stand before your spouse as judge, or your parents, or yourself. Jesus alone will judge you. He will judge your life, and based on your life, your faith will be shown for what it really was. On that day nothing else will matter except for Jesus' declaration concerning your life. On that day many will think, ***I knew this was coming. Why didn't I believe it?!*** You don't have to be this person. You can, like Paul, walk according to this reality, and therefore be assured of what awaits you because of your steadfast service to Christ and His Kingdom.

> "I have fought the good fight, I have finished the race, I have kept the faith. Now there is in store for me the crown of righteousness, which the Lord, the righteous Judge, will award to me on that day—and not only to me, but also to all who have longed for his appearing."
>
> 2 Timothy 4:7,8

The true followers of God's Kingdom have, from the beginning, understood this to be true. If we are going to likewise be heroes of God's Kingdom, we must fear Him.

> "Since you call on a Father who judges each man's work impartially, live your lives as strangers here in reverent fear. "   1 Peter 1:17

> "The fear of the Lord is the beginning of knowledge and wisdom…"
>
> Proverbs 1:7; 9:10

END NOTES:

Main Points:

- Your primary goal should be to please God.
- You should fear God.
- God will judge you on that day.

Questions to Consider:

- If someone was to follow you around for a week or two, would they conclude that you believe that you will one day stand before the judgment seat of Christ? Explain.
- How would the fear of the Lord benefit your personal kingdom?

The Discipline of Study:

Read Hebrews 10:26-31. Many people try to soften this passage or justify it away by traditional teaching. Don't do that. Read it for what it says and allow the reality of Jesus being Judge to penetrate your heart. Record any questions/observations and then answer the questions below:

- How does this passage challenge your thinking?
- How should the realities given here affect your life?
- Compare this verse with Galatians 6:7-8 and allow it to give you additional insight. Paraphrase this verse in Galatians in your own words. What is the main point that Paul is trying to communicate?

The Discipline of Meditation:

This exercise will take two days. Begin in the evening of the first day with meditation upon the memory verse below. You may also want to reread the Parable of the Talents from Matthew 25 and the account of the sheep and the goats. Before you go to bed, pretend that on the evening of the second day you will stand before Jesus to give an account of that day. (This is not too far from the truth.) Live the second day in a constant attitude of Jesus' judgment coming with the twilight. At the end of the day, stand before Him and allow Him to judge you. Afterwards, meditate on the fact that this is going to happen for real at the end of your life. Allow God to open your eyes to the reality of His coming judgment.

The Discipline of Memorization:

1 Peter 1:17

> "Since you call on a Father who judges each man's work impartially, live your lives as strangers here in reverent fear. "

The Discipline of Prayer:

Great Almighty Judge, You are worthy to be feared and exalted, for You are the Judge over all of creation. One day I will stand before You to give an account for the life and stewardship You have given me. On that day, I will understand better than ever that you are Judge. May I not be found wanting. Create in me a holy fear for You, that I might walk in a way that pleases You. To You be the glory. Amen.

CHAPTER 10

THE HEAD OF THE BODY

"And he (Jesus) is the head of the body, the church..." --
Colossians 1:18

"Now you are the body of Christ, and each one of you is a part of it."-
1 Corinthians 12:27

This final characteristic of Christ that we are going to consider is without doubt the most overlooked and misunderstood of all that has yet been mentioned. It is wrapped around words that we use every day, and yet for some reason (the schemes of the Devil perhaps?) we don't seem to apply it at all. Scripture teaches us that we are the body of Christ, and that He is our head. What does this practically mean for us? To answer this, we must first discuss the word *church*.

WHAT IS THE CHURCH?

In Book Three of this series, we discuss the concepts and implications of this chapter at much greater lengths. Here, we will only scratch enough of the surface as is sufficient to help us along. The word that we read in our bible, translated 'church', literally means 'called out' or 'the called-out ones'. Ever since the curse of Adam, God has been calling people out of the darkness of Satan's kingdom and into His Kingdom of light. This is His church. It is a people; a people that form a holy nation (1 Peter 2:9). It is not, as is readily practiced, a building or an institution. (Most of us tend to know this, but we must consider whether or not our actions support it.)

The next question then is this: Why did God make the church? Why did God call us out of the darkness? What was His purpose in doing so? We answered these questions in Book One. He called us out of the darkness so we could fulfill our initial purpose of ruling with Him. According to the passages of scripture above, the form we take in doing this mission is His body. Individually, I am a son of God, made in His image to rule with Him. And through His Spirit, I am able to do amazing things. But I will never accomplish God's goal for my life or for His Kingdom on my own. There are no lone rangers in God's Kingdom. He made us to be a people, joined together as one body. This is the church.

What does it mean for you to immerse yourself in Jesus Christ as the Head of His body? This is a crucial question. And the ramifications are enormous. There are multiple results of this immersion that will radically change your experience in God's Kingdom. We will now briefly discuss these results.

YOU WILL RECOGNIZE THAT YOU ARE A PART OF HIS BODY, AND THAT YOU THEREFORE HAVE A SPECIAL ROLE TO PLAY.

Before you were born, God already knew you. Before He created the world He had already determined what your special gifting and role would be in His body. In the church today, we mainly tend to think of this solely in the context of hired or professional Christian workers. We make comments like, 'God has a calling on that person's life.' This is not a bad thing to say, but what we must realize is that it is true for ever disciple of Christ. If you are a disciple, then God has a specific calling for you. This is why you are one of his 'called out ones'. We also say things like, 'That person is a full-time minister of Christ.' This is also a good saying if we apply it to all of Christ's body. If you are a disciple, then you are a full-time minister of God's Kingdom. You are a part of the body and therefore have a part to play.

> "From him the whole body, joined and held together by every supporting ligament, grows and builds itself up in love, as each part does its work."
>
> Ephesians 4:16

Notice that it says, *as each part does its work*. The body of Christ will not be built up the way God intends it to unless each part does its work. The point is this: **God has a special role for you.** You have a special role that is meant to bless Christ's body. You will never be able to function correctly in this role until you first recognize the need to immerse yourself in your Heavenly Head.

YOU WILL RECOGNIZE THAT THERE IS ONLY ONE BODY, AND WILL THEREFORE DISCARD ANY NEED FOR DIVISION IN THE BODY.

> "The body is a unit, though it is made up of many parts; and though all its parts are many, they form one body."
>
> 1 Corinthians 12:12

How many bodies do we form? Only one. This is so central to the Kingdom of God that one wonders how we have arrived at our current situation. We must remember that our enemy is clever, and that he is a very good deceiver. We must remember also that he loves religion. In Paul's letter to the believers in Corinth, he labels them as carnal, or immature. He did not call them carnal because of gross sin, such as lust or greed or murder. No, the factor for this title was that there were divisions among these believers (1 Cor 1:10-13; 3:1-4). They were creating and classifying different sects within the body of Christ, and for doing so, they were labeled as *worldly*. The body of Christ today has in like manner been divided. There is division after division. There is even division within each division. According to Paul's words to the people of Corinth, this makes us nothing more than mere men. By our division, we lower ourselves to nothing more than just fallen people acting like fallen people. This attitude and practice is completely opposed to the will of our Heavenly Head who prayed that we would be brought to 'complete unity'.

All of the divisions in Christ's body today are derived from one source: the traditions of men. The Sunday service is a perfect example of this. One group prefers liturgy, another doesn't. One group wants traditional music (which used to be considered overly modern and inappropriate in the church) while another group doesn't. If you put these same people on a service project, they would be completely united in service and love. But start talking about what translation of the Bible they use, and fellowship will be broken. This is not what Jesus had in mind when He said, "On this rock I will build my church, and the gates of Hell will not prevail against it." How do we expect to overcome the gates of Hell when we can't overcome a difference or preference regarding Bible translations?

An obvious tradition that is widespread across this globe is that of racial distinction. In my current community, there is one black church gathering, surrounded by multiple white church gatherings. Everyone in the city knows that this is the case, and many of them don't at all see it as a problem. In their eyes, it is culturally acceptable to have a separation of white and black people. And yet in the culture of God's Kingdom, it is far from appropriate and does not at all please God.

Another tradition that separates us today is the doctrines of men. We isolate certain verses in God's word, make a doctrine around it, and then only allow those in agreement with us to have fellowship. Ironically, many of these doctrines have little to no lasting effect on the life of the believer. What is the cure for this? Though it might seem too easy to be true, most of these traditional doctrines would disappear with a simple understanding of the Kingdom of God. The point here is simple: until you immerse yourself in the reality that you are part of one body with one Head, you will never experience the immense blessing of unity in the body.

YOU WILL SEEK TO ASSEMBLE WITH OTHER PARTS OF CHRIST'S BODY.

"Not forsaking the assembling of ourselves together…"

Hebrews 10:25 (KJV)

The bible tells us to, 'not forsake the assembling of ourselves together'. This word *assemble* is crucial when it comes to the body of Christ. Just as many things need assembly, such as a bicycle for example, so does the body of Christ. It needs to be assembled! Consider your own physical body. Is it a good thing that it is assembled? Of course! Without its assembling together, you would die! The question we must consider is this: **When we come together with other disciples, are we an assembled body, or are we a gathering of body parts?**

Something powerful and very beneficial is supposed to happen when disciples come together. You will leave that gathering equipped for good works and built up in love. You will be personally ministered to as a lamb is cared for by his shepherd. If you are not experiencing these things on a regular basis, then only two explanations exists. Either you are out of fellowship with God and others (a very rebellious state of being) or you are not correctly assembling together with other believers. The point here is very clear in God's word: First, if you are not assembling in a way which allows you to contribute to the body, then you are an inactive body part. Second, if you are not being adequately equipped for service in God's Kingdom, then you are not rightly assembling with other Christians. You see, this is not only about immersing yourself in Christ as your Head, but also about immersing yourself in His body.

> "From him the whole body, joined and held together by every supporting ligament, grows and builds itself up in love, as each part does its work."
>
> *Ephesians 4:16*

YOU WILL SEEK OUT THE GUIDANCE OF YOUR HEAVENLY HEAD, SO THAT HE MIGHT SHOW YOU HOW TO FUNCTION.

> "He has lost connection with the Head, from whom the whole body, supported and held together by its ligaments and sinews, grows as God causes it to grow."
>
> *Colossians 2:19*

Connection with the head is necessary for any body part to function. If I cut off my hand, I could try to make it move with my mind, but it would have no effect. It would also hurt the rest of my body. (Something to consider.)

Jesus wants to direct you in the manner of your gifting and contribution to the body. He, through His Spirit, determined what your gifts would be, and He has already mapped out what He wants you to do (Ephesians 2:10). This makes Him, therefore, the only hope you have of fulfilling the goal for which you were specifically made. You must be connected with Him, seeking His will for you in relation to the other members of His body.

THE EXAMPLE OF THOSE YET TO COME

Instead of looking back for an example of this (which we certainly could, for they are many- the church in Acts for instance), I want to inform you of the example that is coming. Jesus, whose body is very much divided and cut apart, is bringing about a restoration of these things we are now discussing. Much of the body of Christ will soon turn away from an obsession with worldly tradition and will reunite under the one banner of Christ. They will become an assembly instead of a gathering. They will each perform their ordained role to which God has called them. This is God's calling for you. And you must respond appropriately.

THE CHALLENGE

> "My prayer is not for them alone. I pray also for those who will believe in me through their message, that all of them may be one, Father, just as you are in me and I am in you. May they also be in us so that the world may believe that you have sent me."
>
> John 17:20,21

This passage is the only time in Scripture that Jesus prays for you and me. His prayer was very specific. He prayed that we (His body) would be one. Don't you think that it is only right for us to make this our number one priority? This is, after all, the will of our King! He wants us to be one body with one Head. We must therefore throw aside all of the meaningless traditions that divide us. Let me be clear, there are certain doctrines and teachings that are essential, and if not agreed upon, should cause division. I want to challenge you however that of the fifty things that cause division in the church today, only three of them are essentials and the rest are traditions. There are only three essential issues from which everything else flows. These are God, His Kingdom, and His message. If the church can, by God's grace, get these correct, then unity will flow like a river. Ironically, it is easy for us to focus on everything but these three things. You must do your part: continue to seek first the Kingdom of God, let go of all traditions that bring division, and allow your Heavenly Head to grow you up in your place in His body.

END NOTES:

Main Points:

- The word translated 'church' means 'called-out ones'.
- The church is a group of people whom God has called and taken out of the darkness.
- The church is the body of Christ.
- Every member of Christ's body has a specific role.
- If you are not assembling in a way which allows you to contribute to the body, then you are an inactive body part.
- If you are not being adequately equipped for service in God's Kingdom, then you are not rightly assembling with other Christians.
- Jesus is the head of His body.

Questions to Consider:

- When you think of the word *church*, what usually comes to mind?
- I told you that before you were born, God had a special role for you to play as a member of His body. What causes you to either believe or doubt this statement?
- When you gather with other Christians, do you see yourselves as a body that is assembled, or as a gathering of body parts? Please explain.
- What paradigms in your thinking were challenged by this teaching?

The Discipline of Study:

Read through Romans 12:3-8 and 1 Corinthians 12:4-20 and Ephesians 4:11-16 and answer the following questions…

- What insights do you gain from Romans 12:4?

- According to 1 Corinthians 12:7, what is the purpose for the gifts?

- According to 1 Corinthians 12:11, who determines who gets what gift?

- According to Ephesians 4:11,12, what is the purpose for the five gifts mentioned there?

- How does the description given in 1 Corinthians 14:26-33 align with or contradict your current gatherings?

The Discipline of Meditation:

As you do normal daily activities (get the mail, eat dinner, tidy your home, etc…) try to do so without the use of a needed body part. This might mean walking with only one leg, or eating dinner left handed, or opening the mail box with your elbows. Allow yourself a chance to experience the frustration of a body that is not working together in harmony. Imagine also the frustration of people whose body parts will not respond to their brains wishes. (For some people, this is an everyday experience.) Then, after some time of frustration, allow your body to walk together and focus on the joy of an assembled body. Allow the Spirit of God to open your eyes up to the insight of this biblical analogy. Ask God to strengthen your connection to the Head as you grow more in Him.

The Discipline of Memorization:

Ephesians 4:16

> "From him the whole body, joined and held together by every supporting ligament, grows and builds itself up in love, as each part does its work."

The Discipline of Prayer:

I thank You, Lord Jesus Christ, that You have given me the privilege to be part of Your body. I pray that I would fulfill the role that you have given me. May Your body be one body, just as you desired in the beginning. Guard me against the traditions of men. Help me to not walk according to any tradition, but instead to walk according to your Spirit and your Kingdom. Amen.

CHAPTER 11

THE HOLY SPIRIT

"And with that he breathed on them and said, "Receive the Holy Spirit."

--John 20:22

The Holy Spirit has been called by Francis Chan the **Forgotten God**. Unfortunately, this is an appropriate title considering that most church going people live their lives virtually void of any real interaction with the Holy Spirit. What is more, most spiritually minded Christians are quicker to see the Holy Spirit as a tool or thing instead of the person of God Himself. Scripture is very clear that the Holy Spirit is God. He was involved in creation, the resurrection of Jesus, and our regeneration. It is for this reason that Jesus implores us to be immersed in the Holy Spirit.

One of the names for Jesus is Immanuel, which means **God with us**. The Holy Spirit is **God in us**. Today, through His Spirit, God is not only with us, but also in us. Our spirit and God's Holy Spirit are in relationship together.

This is why we are able to live the life that God desires- we participate in the divine nature (2nd Peter 1:3).

When it comes to immersing ourselves in the Spirit, it is best to begin with who the Spirit is in terms of our relationship with Him. The reason this is so revealing is that with every aspect of His activity we discover another way to immerse ourselves in Him. Who is the Holy Spirit? Jesus answered this in many wonderful ways:

GUIDE

> "But when he, the Spirit of truth, comes, he will guide you into all truth."
>
> *John 16:13*

There are many different contexts in our activity where a guide is useful. Most of us will initially think of a tour guide. My wife and I recently visited Longhorn Cavern State Park where we had a guide lead us through more than one mile of underground tunnels. There is much we can draw from this example. What gave this man the authority or the right to call himself a guide? It was his knowledge and experience of the caverns, as well as the authority given him by the park, that made him worthy of the title. Within the context of Longhorn Caverns this man was virtually all-knowing. He was an expert. He was able therefore to guide us down the safest paths. He was also able to teach us many wonderful things and instruct us concerning many important details. So what was our attitude toward our guide? We listened to him. We asked questions. We obeyed his instruction. And our overall experience therefore was greatly altered from if we'd done our own thing.

It is the same with the Holy Spirit. He is our Expert Guide. He has all of the answers and all of the instruction. We have the opportunity to immerse ourselves in Him by seeking His guidance and responding appropriately. Remember also that the Holy Spirit's context of expertise is not narrowed down to a small framework such as a cavern or a certain aspect of life. If I were to take my cavern guide three miles down the road to the German castle that overlooks the city of Kingsland, he would no longer be my guide because he would be out of his field of expertise. Not so with the Holy Spirit. His field of expertise is everywhere and everything. He is not only the best guide for going to heaven, but also concerning life today.

> "I will instruct you and teach you in the way you should go; I will counsel you and watch over you."
>
> Psalm 32:8

To immerse ourselves in the Holy Spirit is to see Him as our Guide, and therefore seek His guidance continually. As you go throughout your day, there He is, guiding you along. As you think through things, there He is, giving you insight about how to reason and respond concerning certain situations. He is the all-powerful, all-knowing, all-present Guide, and He desires to guide you. The question is: ***Will you seek His guidance?***

THE EXAMPLE OF JESUS

> "Then Jesus was led by the Spirit…"
>
> Matthew 4:1

As already discussed, Jesus lived a life that was 100% guided by the Holy Spirit. He didn't only do this to be a good example to us, but also because He had too! The only way for Jesus to live the life He did was for the Spirit to be guiding

Him continually. Jesus didn't see this as a weakness, but rather as a privilege. The Kingdom of God is not about independence in living, but rather dependence upon the Spirit of God.

COUNSELOR

> "But I tell you the truth: It is for your good that I am going away. Unless I go away, the Counselor will not come to you; but if I go, I will send him to you."
>
> *John 16:7*

How often do you look to others for counsel? For most of us, in some form or another, this happens daily. Whether it is a friend, spouse, substance, or a system of thinking, we all look to something or someone else for advice in the midst of trial. Many of these things we run to for counsel are not bad in and of themselves. Yet, they can often give counsel contrary to God's Kingdom. There is the world's counsel and God's counsel and they are opposed to each other.

Consider how much our culture values counsel. In our nation there are thousands upon thousands of people whose full time occupation is giving other people, usually strangers, counsel. And many of these counselors have specific areas of expertise. There are marriage counselors, financial counselors, children counselors, as well as psychological counselors. And many people will spend large sums of money and will put into practice all the words of their counselor because they see them as qualified.

The Holy Spirit is the best counselor in existence. He is so good in fact that you can't rightly put Him on the same level as human or even angelic counselors. His fields of expertise are boundless. His knowledge is limitless. And He is available 24/7. It is not bad to get the advice of others. But before we go to other people we should go to the Holy Spirit. I wonder how many unneeded conversations and actions have taken place because we didn't first go to our Counselor, given to us by God. This then is what it means to immerse ourselves in our Counselor; **when we need counsel we go to Him**. This simple practice will be life altering if done well and regularly.

THE EXAMPLE OF JESUS

> "One of those days Jesus went out to a mountainside to pray, and spent the night praying to God. When morning came, he called his disciples to him and chose twelve of them, whom he also designated apostles..."
>
> Luke 6:12

Why did Jesus spend the night praying to God? It was because He needed counsel. He knew that it was time for Him to pick the men who would change the world. Notice that Jesus didn't spend all night polling his peers or taking applications. When we need counsel, we should always go to the Spirit first. This is why prayer is the chief discipline of the disciple; we need guidance, therefore, we pray.

COMFORTER

The word translated *Counselor* in John 16:7 could also be translated *Comforter*. Being able to find comfort in this life is a gift from God. It is part of His common grace given to all of mankind. How often do you seek out comfort? I'm sure that if you looked into it you would conclude that this is a daily activity. We can find comfort in both people and things. For many people their spouse or best friend is a common source of comfort. In the midst of pain they will seek out a trusting ear or a familiar shoulder to rest upon. Often our source of comfort becomes things such as food, substances, pleasure, or entertainment. We are stressed out or burdened so we just *veg* on the couch and put in a movie (and grab a chocolate bar while we are at it). Many addictions form from a need for comfort. Why is this? Because God made us to be people who need comfort. He made us to be a people that must look outside of ourselves for help. This is not a bad thing. It is good to find comfort in others (in an appropriate way and with appropriate measure).

But again we see that in the Holy Spirit we have the best comforter in existence. He is our Comforter. And He invites us to immerse ourselves in Him as such. How do we do this? Simple. ***Whenever we need comfort, we go to Him.*** Understand, just as with all of these names of the Holy Spirit, I'm not saying it is wrong to go to others. This is rather a question of who we go to first. And it is also a question that addresses how to rid ourselves of the things we run to that are sinful and inappropriate.

Unfortunately, training ourselves to run to the Holy Spirit for comfort can be very difficult and often frustrating. This is because our main experience regarding comfort is not spiritual, but rather physical. This world has trained us to seek out instant physical gratification to cope with our pain. Physical comfort, such as a hug, is a very good thing. The Spirit will often use others, such as a friend or spouse, to minister to us in a physical way. In addition to this, the Holy Spirit desires to minister to our spirits, and we must therefore allow Him the opportunity to do so. We must allow Him to teach us how to receive His spiritual comfort. This will often be through a thought or scripture that encourages us. We can also receive the Spirit's comfort by simply sensing and enjoying His presence with us. We will often speak of spending time with God, and yet for most people, it is extremely one sided. We read, we talk, and we write, but we don't take the time to be still and allow Him to minister to us.

THE EXAMPLE OF JESUS

> "And being in anguish, he prayed more earnestly, and his sweat was like drops of blood falling to the ground."
>
> Luke 22:44

On the night before His crucifixion, Jesus was in more despair than any disciple will ever experience. Why is this? Because in addition to the physical pain that was approaching, He was also going to be spiritually separated and forsaken by His Father. And what was His reaction? He prayed more earnestly. Jesus never ran to the comfort of this world. He rightly knew that the best source of comfort was the Spirit of God. Do we share this same conviction?

TEACHER & REMINDER

> "But the Counselor, the Holy Spirit, whom the Father will send in my name, will teach you all things and will remind you of everything I have said to you."
>
> John 14:26

Just like there are many counselors in this world, there are even more teachers. And this is wonderful, for teachers are needed in every realm of life. I am a teacher to my children, trying to show them how to follow the narrow path that leads to life. We all have teachers. But the question remains, **Who is our primary Teacher?** Who is our ultimate authority on all things? Jesus said that the Holy Spirit will teach us. And not only will He teach us, but He will teach us all things. He has all of the answers. The question is, what do you want to know? Do you want to know how to be good spouse, parent, and friend? Do you want to know how to be successful in your vocation? Do you want to know how to take good care of your body, your temple that God has given you? Do you want to know how to invest your money wisely? Do you want to know how to handle conflict? All of these questions and any others that you could come up with are all questions that the Holy Spirit can answer. **He is Teacher**. How do you immerse yourself in Him as Teacher? You learn from Him. You sit at His feet and listen. You look within His Scripture and search. And you do what He tells you. Simple, right? The Christian life is simple. So simple that a child can live it. You and I must think like children do. If my son or daughter has a question, who do they go to? To them, it is a simple manner of reasoning. **Dad knows the answer. I'm going to ask Him.** It should be the same for us. **What should I do about this situation? The Holy Spirit knows. I'll ask Him.** And not only will He teach me, but He will also remind me of what I've been learning.

THE EXAMPLE OF JESUS

> "...everything that I learned from my Father I have made known to you."
>
> John 15:15

As previously mentioned, the common consensus in the church today is that Jesus knew everything because He was God. Yet here we see that Jesus did indeed live His life as one of us, and therefore need to learn how to live. This teaching from His Father was no doubt given to Him by the Spirit.

THE CHALLENGE

Now that we have listed only a few names of the Holy Spirit, I want you to ask yourself this question: ***Who do I go to for these needs?*** Who is my main teacher? Don't answer based on what you know to be the right answer. Answer rather based on your experience. When you have a question, who do you go to? Who is your main counselor? When you need advice, who do you initially seek out? Who or what is your main comforter? When you are down and out, or when you are stressed and tired, who or what do you go to? For nearly all people, the answers to these questions will involve spouses, friends, co-workers, professional therapist, as well as worldly things from food, sinful activity, and substance abuse. The question we must then ask as we step back and look at our answers is, ***Who is my guide?*** The sobering reality in my own life when I asked this question was that the world was my guide. And yet this doesn't have to be the case. God in His grace has given us Himself, the Holy Spirit, to be our Guide in this life. But He isn't going to force it upon us. We have the choice to ether immerse ourselves in our Guide or not.

END NOTES:

Main Points:

- We need guidance, counsel, comfort, and teaching.
- Whatever we run to for these things defines who or what we are submerging ourselves into.
- The Holy Spirit is the best Guide ever.

Questions to Consider:

- Who or what do you run to (first) when you need guidance? Counsel? Comfort? Insight?
- As you look at your answers to the above questions, what do you immerse yourself in more, the world or the Spirit?
- Is the church teaching us to go to God first? What are some of the more common things that the church puts before God in regards to our daily need for guidance?
- List some insights/challenges that this chapter gives you:

The Discipline of Study:

In this chapter we used Jesus as an example of how to walk within each of the qualities of the Holy Spirit given (Guide, Counselor, Comforter, Teacher, Reminder). For each of these characteristics, try to find examples in the Bible of people who did not go to God first.

Read Acts 15:22-29 and Acts 16:6-10. What phrases in these accounts gives us a perfect example of the point of this chapter? What kind of difference did these peoples' connection with the Holy Spirit make in the lives of others?

The Discipline of Meditation:

Imagine that you have a personal trainer that is with you every day. He (or she) is very skilled and wise and knowledgeable. Imagine this person correcting you and teaching you and training you in all kinds of different contexts of life. Meditate on what kind of impact this would make on your life (it wouldn't just slightly change you, but would instead bring huge amounts of discipline and wisdom and character to your life!)

Now meditate on the fact that this is what you have in the Holy Spirit. Ask God to help you to believe this and therefore be more acclimated to the Spirit. Ask your Guide questions about your life; what you need to change? What you can do better? What you're doing well? Then listen.

The Discipline of Memorization:

John 16:13

> "But when he, the Spirit of truth, comes, he will guide you into all truth."

John 14:26

> "But the Counselor, the Holy Spirit, whom the Father will send in my name, will teach you all things and will remind you of everything I have said to you."

Psalm 32:8

> "I will instruct you and teach you in the way you should go; I will counsel you and watch over you."

The Discipline of Prayer:

Holy Spirit, You are my Guide and my Teacher. I submit myself to You and Your guiding hand. Open my eyes to You and Your ministry which is at work within me. Help me to practice Your presence more and more. Amen.

Made in the USA
Monee, IL
23 September 2021